Collected Poems 1958–1982

COLLECTED POEMS
1958–1982

George MacBeth

Hutchinson

London   Sydney   Auckland   Johannesburg

© George MacBeth 1989

This edition first published in
Great Britain by Hutchinson, an
imprint of Century Hutchinson Ltd
Brookmount House, 62–65 Chandos Place,
London WC2N 4NW

Century Hutchinson Australia (Pty) Ltd
80 Alfred Street, Milsons Point, Sydney 2061, Australia

Century Hutchinson New Zealand Limited
PO Box 40–086, Glenfield, Auckland 10,
New Zealand

Century Hutchinson South Africa (Pty) Ltd
PO Box 337, Berglvei, 2012 South Africa

British Library Cataloguing in Publication Data
MacBeth, George
    Collected Poems, 1958–1982
    1. Poetry in English, 1945– – Text
    I Title
    821.914

ISBN 0 09 173765 6

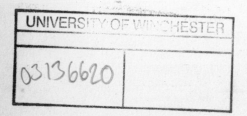

Penny's

Contents

Foreword

In selecting and arranging these poems I have attempted to recover a chronology masked in previous volumes. The earliest poem here, 'The Drawer', was written late in 1958, the latest, 'To Alexander, Sleeping', late in 1982. The poems between these two are arranged roughly, but not strictly, in the order in which they were composed. I have sometimes compromised chronology, even when I could remember it, by placing near to each other poems in similar forms or on similar themes. Nothing is present from *A War Quartet, Lusus, The Cleaver Garden* or *Anatomy of a Divorce*, but all of my other fourteen books of verse have made their contribution. One or two titles have been altered, but otherwise the text is largely unchanged. I hope the collection as a whole will reveal interests and patterns in a way that is clear and helpful. A poet nearing sixty expects neither pardon nor quarter, but the ache for understanding grows with time. 'I see what you mean' begins to seem a nicer piece of praise than 'I like what you're doing'.

The Drawer

Their belongings were buried side by side
In a shallow bureau drawer. There was her
Crocodile handbag, letters, a brooch,
All that was in the bedside cupboard
And a small green jar she'd had for flowers.

My father's were in an envelope:
A khaki lanyard, crushed handkerchief,
Twelve cigarettes, a copying pencil,
All he had on him when he was killed
Or all my mother wanted to keep.

I put them together seven years ago.
Now that we've moved, my wife and I,
To a house of our own, I've taken them out.
Until we can find another spare drawer
They're packed in a cardboard box in the hall.

So this dead, middle-aged, middle-class man
Killed by a misfired shell, and his wife
Dead of cirrhosis, have left one son
Aged nine, aged nineteen, aged twenty-six,
Who has buried them both in a cardboard box.

The Passport

Cleaning out old junk, I find
My father's passport, with his picture
Smudged with ink. The mauve-pink paper,
My name signed in his neat writing,
Eden's name there, make it strange.

He used it once, went on business
To Düsseldorf the year of Munich,
Brought me back a clockwork donkey
I still have and saw the war
Coming, which he fought in. Turning

The stiff pages in my hands, I almost
Feel his long-boned hands again
Over my child's hands. I wonder
What he'd think of my passport,
Wine-stained, full of stamps, uncancelled?

His eyes, questioning, look out
From under brushed-back hair. This man will
Never know I've been to Munich
Nor that our side won the war
Between our two journeys, our

Two lives. This draughtsman, born
At Overton in Lanarkshire
Late in 1904, whose height
It says is five foot nine, whose eyes
Are hazel, hair dark brown, is dead.

The Compasses

Baroque-handled and sharp
With blunt lead in their lips
And their fluted legs together
My father's compasses
Lie buried in this flat box.

I take it out of its drawer,
Snap old elastic bands
And rub the frayed leatherette:
It smells faintly of smoke:
The broken hinges yawn.

As I level the case to look
A yellowed protractor claps
Against black-papered board,
Sliding loose in the lid
Behind a torn silk flap.

I look in the base at the dusty
Velvet cavities:
Dead-still, stiff in the joints
And side by side they lie
Like armoured knights on a tomb.

One by one I lift
Them out in the winter air
And wipe some dust away:
Screw back their gaping lips
And bend the rigid knees.

In an inch of hollowed bone
Two cylinders of lead

17

Slither against each other
With a faint scurrying sound.
I lay them carefully back

And close the case. In Crookes
My father's bones are scattered
In a measured space of ground:
Given his flair for drawing
These compasses should be there

Not locked away in a box
By an uninstructed son
But like an Egyptian king's
Ready shield and swords
Beside his crumbling hand.

The Miner's Helmet

My father wore it working coal at Shotts
When I was one. My mother stirred his broth
And rocked my cradle with her shivering hands
While this black helmet's long-lost miner's lamp
Showed him the road home. Through miles of coal
His fragile skull, filled even then with pit-props,
Lay in a shell, the brain's blue-printed future
Warm in its womb. From sheaves of saved brown paper,
Baring an oval into weeks of dust,
I pull it down: its laced straps move to admit
My larger brows; like an abdicated king's
Gold crown of thirty years ago, I touch it

18

With royal fingers, feel its image firm –
Hands grown to kings' hands calloused on the pick,
Feet slow like kings' feet on the throneward gradient
Up to the coal-face – but the image blurs
Before it settles: there were no crusades.
My father died a draughtsman, drawing plans
In an airy well-lit office above the ground
Beneath which his usurpers, other kings,
Reigned by the fallen helmet he resigned
Which I inherit as a concrete husk.
I hand it back to gather dust on the shelf.

The Tin

Its odd inscription caught my eye
Beside the scales: those words 'cream toffees'
In dented gilt across bashed silver
Drove me to lift the lid and look

At what I knew would still be there:
That hammer with a grimed oak handle,
That broken hacksaw, that rusted file,
That Woolworth's chisel bent in the middle,

That wriggle of nails, nuts, bolts and screws.
I tipped them out. The tin looked bare
On the swabbed floor; and I felt moved
With sudden grief for the bright void

My face hung in. I felt as if
The tin's caved sides were drained of breath:

As if there were some vacuum
Inside its walls, inside my skin,

That ached to be fulfilled with care
And swell with hope. But those bent sides
Accused my cold reflected eyes
Of what they knew I'd not yet done

And never would. In awkward rage
I flung the tools back in their place
And closed the lid, and shut my mind,
On guilt I couldn't put in words.

A Death in the North

The fire leaps in the living-room. I poke
Its dying flames. Tar-blackened trucks with coal
Cluttle past the back-room window clagged with soot.
Wheels block the snow-bound farm with mottled cows.

Black milk, white anthracite – where two bloods ran
From pit and furrow – mark their mingling lines:
Hers with blue eyes cold-blow-lamped by the wind
In cheeks filed red from forking swedes in hail;

His with that swamp-rat face from hacking slate
And shoulders hunched from years in pinching seams.
In front the Roman road runs straight as iron
Between the North Sea and the Norsemen's graves

A measured mile. There winged heels flayed the pitch
From bevelled stones where centuries raked the Picts
Across that rambling dyke like sheaves of hay.
Those pickaxe noses, that sea-eagle's beak,

Ravage the vision with a dwindling rage.
I see one's tears, another's tightening lips
At that hook-face held rigid for its course
In slow triumph along the bowing road

Towards its final blaze beyond the pits.
Far off above the farm I count the crows.
At the front gate I hear a car's doors close.
I wave away that polished fleet of Rolls

To coast the Roman road: this rigid man
Whose brows I touch – bare flesh like marzipan
Sealed up in golden wrapping – stretched in state
Like a stone flag to keep the cars in line

South from the mining village to the sea.
A bleak wind from the pit-wheels chills the room.
In the black grate his boots are still burning,
Melting leather mingling with white ash.

St Andrew's

Here in my tight suit, Sunday after Sunday,
I'd shiver in the draughty oblong hall.
(The fire-bomb-gutted church was never used

Except by children or for some church play
That needed ruins.) Here my pimpled skin

Wrinkled in prayer when I propped my head
On my poised fingers: forms of words worn thin
Helped me to remember what should be said.
I'd bend beside my mother, gangling, tall.
I prayed for faith, but felt that God refused.

Let me look back. I'm there in my rough chair,
Bare legs on sharp straw, sucking buttermint
Slipped in my fidgeting hands by fur-gloved hands.
I'm wondering when the intercession-prayer
Will end. More prayers, intimations, hymns

Flounce leisurely on. I watch bulged offering bags
Shuttle between deacons. Touched coins chink. Stiff limbs
Ease. The soft mouths, whose belly-velvet sags,
Gape for warmed silver, trickling out by dint
Of pressed appeals for 'our missions in far lands'.

The lesson booms out. James McClusky's black
Bony razor-headed bust above the bible
Strops his Highland vowels. Quick Scottish wives
Nudge their slumped husbands. Folded arms, feet slack
On loud planks correct themselves. The Book

Quietly shuts, gold leaves flutter. Towards
The back of the hall the text from Habbakuk
Re-echoes. The draped lectern's tasselled cords
Jerk to swung robes. The minister turns: the table
Quakes to beat fists condemning our distracted lives.

Let me look forward. As I grate on boards
I bump the lion-mouthed mahogany throne

He'd hunch in. It's ground by lecturers now. Dead flowers
Droop on the flat piano from which the Lord's
Thundering praises were wrung. I cough and choke

In dust (it's little played now) and stoop through
To the new church: too elegant in oak
For my taste. I advance to our old pew
Through pipe-warmed air. I sit down, scrape fresh stone
With dragging nailed heels. Here, while quarter-hours

Flake from the tower, I stop. My child's belief
(I now believe) was a Scots exile's; gone
With loosened roots. When the sick wish returns
For the lost country, the dream-Scotland grief
Was noble in, I clutch at *things*, plain things

I've lifted to symbols: compasses, a brooch,
Photographs, draughtsman's T-squares, opal rings.
My faith's planted where prayers can't encroach.
I've grown past God-roots. Why, then, back there on
That warm pew do they prick me? Something turns

Time back. It's Easter Day. I see moved plates
Of diced white bread, starched linen someone clears.
The plates clink closer. Furtively, I choose
Christ's body and blood. The hushed young elder waits,
Then catfoots on. And now I'm swallowing wine

From a glass thimble, rolling the lifeless bread
On my living tongue. I'm keyed for some sure sign
Of something miraculous. Eyes blink; my head
Lifts; and I stare at grown men shedding tears
And my own goosefleshed knees, blue with a bruise.

Remembering Greystones

What did I learn at Greystones, my first school?
Something from clay. I don't mean garden clay
My father sliced like fudge-lumps, broken fudge-lumps,
With a steel spade's-edge. I mean clay for playing with,
Squelching-wet, white stuff: clay mashed flat like dough
On sweating palms; dried hard in brittle spindles
Between slow fingers; caked on backs of hands
Plunged wrist-deep into whitewash in grey clay-bins
Jammed in an art-room's corner to cludge it out.
Clay taught me filth. And what did tar teach me,
Stuck to my shoes' greyed lozenge-patterned rubbers
On the baked asphalt of our melting playground?
Tar taught what fire does. Before war broke out
I'd seen a trapped boy terrified by fire
Forced by six others in a smoke-filled cellar
And kept there coughing, choked with swirling ash;
And another crouching with his tight knees browned
With diarrhoea, blubbing behind the backs
At being nicknamed 'stinker'.
My uncle died floundering through Belgian sludge
In the First World War: my father died in fire
Charred in a Sheffield blitz. Through filth and smoke
Forgotten links with those blood-ridden soldiers
Educate my will. In clay and tar
Two wars collide: fouled bodies from my childhood,
War as the art-room clay, as playground tar,
Sharpens to that boy choking, that boy jeered at:
Tears, diarrhoea: what being burned, being dirty means:
That's what I learned at Greystones, my first school.

The Knives

I own four knives that were made for killing. They decorate
    my house. In romantic moods
I picture myself accosting a burglar with one of them. First, a
    Victorian bayonet. This
One took a hell of a lot of guts to handle, I'll bet. It's a heavy
    thing. You can wrench

It in and out of its sheath, but it calls for a certain amount of
    sweat. I've crossed the two
I think of next like swords on my dining-room mantelpiece.
    First, a diminutive fruit-knife, marked
'Enthumion', Greek for 'a gift', for the classical tourist: a neat
    little scissor for slitting

An adam's apple. Some kind of juice has rusted the crescent
    steel. It sticks when it slides
From its wooden sheath. And second, my Scottish dirk. It's
    encased in a frayed-cardboard, Cameron-
Tartan holder. I clean its hilt's chased silver once in about six
    months. The dirt's

Ingrained like ash in the curling crevices. The blade has a
    diamond section. It's sharpened
On both sides like an axe. Given a cool head and a steady
    hand you could use
It for peeling potatoes. I don't. The last one's a lightweight
    ivory 'Chinese' throwing-knife. The tip's

Broken off. And there's dried blood on the blunt edge and the
    words 'Meet Me at Maules'
In copper-plate. There are thirty-eight uneven slots notched in
    the hilt. All men

It's killed, I'd like to think. I wonder why I preserve these four
　　　not very important knives

I never use or clean. To give them space for decay in a decent
　　　slowness? In guilt
For a cushioned, inhibited life? I avoid their implications:
　　　they decorate my house
Through which I walk in the warmth of my five electric fires
　　　secure from the need to kill.

The Bird

When I got home
Last night I found
A bird the cat
Had brought into the house
On the kitchen floor.

It wasn't dead.
It looked as if
It was, at first.
There were some feathers lying
Against the wall:

The bird itself
With its wings folded
Lay and stared.
It didn't move.
I picked it up:

Quivering like a clockwork
Toy in my hand
I carried it out
Into the yard
And put it down

In a slice of light
From the door. I lifted
A long broom
By the handle near to
The head and struck

The bird four times.
The fourth time it
Didn't move.
Blood, in a stringy
Trickle, blotched

The white concrete.
I edged the remains
Up with a red
Plastic shovel.
Lifting it through

The house to the cellar
I tipped it out
In the dust-bin along with
Snakes of fluff
And empty soup-tins.

When I emptied the tea leaves
This morning I saw
The bird I killed
Leaning its head
On a broken egg-shell.

The Wasps' Nest

All day to the loose tile behind the parapet
The droning bombers fled: in the wet gutter
Belly-upwards the dead were lying, numbed
By October cold. And now the bloat queen,
Sick-orange, with wings draped, and feelers trailing,
Like Helen combing her hair, posed on the ledge
Twenty feet above the traffic. I watched, just a foot
From her eyes, very glad of the hard glass parting
My pressed human nose from her angry sting
And her heavy power to warm the cold future
Sunk in unfertilized eggs. And I thought: if I reached
And inched this window open, and cut her in half
With my unclasped penknife, I could exterminate
An unborn generation. All next summer,
If she survives, the stepped roof will swarm
With a jam of striped fighters. Therefore, this winter
In burning sulphur in their dug-out hangars
All the bred wasps must die. Unless I kill her.
So I balanced assassination with genocide
As the queen walked on the ledge, a foot from my eyes
In the last sun of the year, the responsible man
With a cold nose, who knew that he must kill,
Coming to no sure conclusion, nor anxious to come.

A Child's Garden

Who was here. Before his cat
Washed and rose. Without his shoes
Who inched outside while someone's hat
Made a noise. Light feet helped. Who's.

Whose are these eggs? Ladybird's.
Hard like crumbs of sleep. She flies
Off to help who find some words
For sounds and things. Who's two puffed eyes

Tug at flowers now for bees
Tucked away. Some try to hide
In pouting fox-gloves' jugs. Who sees
Their fat bear's thighs, though, wedged inside

Scouring honey. Look! Rare stones
In lupin leaves. Who's flapping gown
Shakes them all out. Ow! Who's bones
Aren't awake, make who fall down

Biting earth. Who hears a sound.
Whose are these wet softish hairs
Brushing someone's mouth? Can bound
As quick as you. Whoosh! Peter scares

A thin bird. Zip! Squawk! Its beak
Almost nipped who's fattest worm
Head and tail. Who hears him squeak
Through the grass: who sees him squirm

Down a hole. Who wants to kiss
His frightened worm. Who's coolish knees

29

Push him up to clematis
He thinks it's called. It makes him sneeze.

Gooseflesh comes. Who's bare toes rake
Up oily slugs. Who wants to hop,
Skip. Who's flopping tassels make
Ants run. Who hears his crispies pop.

Amelia's Will

Where was Amelia's Will, and what was in it?
After the funeral, but not long after,
These were the questions her four sisters pondered
And three came to Amelia's cottage demanding
Answers to. Anne came with her sharp wit,
Alice with a hammer, Agnes with paper. Gwen,
Gwen thought there *was* no Will, and what was in it,
If there had been one, would have shocked them sadly,
So Gwen just came to watch.

               Well, now, the search for it
Started quite well. First they evacuated
A ton of anthracite from the cellar, some pounds
Of coffee, flour, snuff, sugar and other powders
(Into which paper might have been ground) from the larder
And a quantity of ash from the kitchen grate.
That layer of dust along the banister
Gwen pointed out, none thought seemed thick enough,
So it was left. All yielded no results,

Though examined with great care through powerful lenses
For the imprint of invisible ink or fingers.

Where could the Will be? They grew violent.
Alice knocked bricks out from the front porch. Anne
Pulled at hall plaster with implacable anger.
And Agnes snapped four planks in the kitchen floor.
But no Will could be found, nor one deduced
From these concrete particulars, or others
Produced by such firm violence of three sisters.

Gwen kept her counsel. In the rocking chair
Amelia loved to rock in by her window
That overlooked the lake, Gwen knitted socks
With pins she'd brought to soothe her flurried nerves.
They were soon needed. Anne lit a fire in
The dining room and burned Amelia's nightie.
Alice shook all her books out and poured water
Over what Gwen thought was a fine collection
Of works on cookery. And Agnes screamed
Improper words no decent girl would whisper
In Gwen's opinion.

                  But things went too far
When cowed Saltpetre had to spring for life
To the linen cupboard to escape Anne's murderous
Jab with a carver. 'How could *he* have swallowed
Amelia's Will?' Gwen cried. 'Be reasonable.
Why must you all behave like mad beasts? Really.'

But her three sisters in frustrated rage
No longer sought Amelia's Will. Gwen's blood,
Sweet blood of reason, pleased their palates more
Than absent paper bound in scarlet ribbon.
So Anne tipped back Gwen's graceful rocking chair

And broke her spine. And Alice cut her up.
And Agnes found, set slantwise in her spleen,
A dart of paper, their Amelia's Will,
Which said: 'I leave my sisters all I have,
Anne shall have Gwen, and Alice Anne . . .'
                                    But here,
Concluding what would happen just in time
To greet Anne's body with a grim composure,
Agnes broke off, and snipped the Will in two.

So two old ladies with a cowed red cat
Spend nights in Devon with their bedroom lights on
Glaring like polished silver at each other.

Mildred

Mildred, our batty cousin, 's been staying with us
Over the weekend. I'm worn out. On Friday
When Mummy and Daddy went to fetch her she wouldn't
Walk downstairs. Mummy said, 'Come on, Mildred,
Let's pretend we're bride and groom (shall we?)
And Daddy can be the bridesmaid.' It's always games
To make her do things, childish silly games
I'm sick to death of. She won't do anything
Without persuading. Do you know that twice
When the doctor made an appointment she was out?
Or she wouldn't see him. He'd gone specially
As a favour to us, too. Is she absent-minded
Or just contrary? Well, we don't know which
So we're keeping her locked up at home till she's seen

The psychiatrist on Thursday. Then she'll go home
Or into a home. Her body's cracking up,
Hospital might be better. She's had two strokes.
She's fifty-eight, but she moves as if she was ninety.
And she talks in this infuriating voice
You can't make head or tail of half the time
It's so slurred and slow. Then she's got kidney trouble
So you can imagine the state her flat's in.
No char would stay. And she's so bloody selfish
She'll fly off the handle at the least complaint
Or interference. 'Why can't I — — come down
To the drawing — — room and meet — — people?' This
                                                    morning
She wouldn't dress. Mummy had to put on
All her clothes: every single stitch.
And there's her money. The lawyer said for weeks
She's been drawing twenty pounds out every day
And then spending it. She bought a bubble car.
She bought this beautiful blue starred lino.
She buys yoghurt. We found twenty bottles
Of yoghurt piled up under her bed: all empty.
And about fifteen more unopened, half in
Half out of the fridge. All going bad, some stinking.
She'll spend a pound on lunch. At Coronelli's
This restaurant she goes to she leaves a pound on the table
And just walks out. I don't know what she's doing.
She'll sit there in the dining room after dinner
Staring ahead of her into empty space
Without looking at anything or moving.
Perhaps she thinks she's back in the theatre.
Theatres are what she's crazy about. Her husband
Victor was manager of the Globe. She goes
Four times a week to the pictures, sits in the front row
Wearing her best clothes, claps when the film's over.
We don't want to interfere: but the neighbours

Just take advantage. As things are she can't
Live on her own, though. And you couldn't have anyone
Living in: she takes such violent
Dislikes to people. She had this Italian woman
Marcellina, once. One day she actually
Threw her out: bundled her out of the door
With all her bags. She was the only one
Who was doing Mildred good. She made her work,
Help clean the place up. Ugh! I pity Granny
Having to sleep in her bed again. She's worse
Than Hank. I hope to God they find some grounds
For doing something definite on Thursday.
If we don't get her certified I'll go mad.

A Confession

Was it alive? I often asked myself
And avoided the answer. I called it something cooking,
Curled up and rising, soft shapeless matter
Stuck to my greased sides waiting to be born.
But once or twice in the small hours I lay thinking
That it could feel things: it was warm in its wet cave,
Swimming and feeding like a baby shrimp there;
And then the hard cold inrush of its killer,
Saw-teeth, threshing fins, cascading water,
And the soul spat like a bubble out of its head,
Three months old. I don't know when they're shaped
Like things you can see are children. I was afraid
To look the books up. I've imagined monsters
At three months: or at best like pancake men,

34

Things from a dream, radiation monsters.
Under the anaesthetic I dreamed nothing.
But one night for the pain they gave me morphia.
I had a strange dream then, worse than a nightmare.
I was in the baby: do you follow me? *in* it.
I'd felt them pull it out: then it grew huge,
Filled the small ward, it was throbbing bloody matter
Soft inside like a cooling hot-cross bun,
And I was in the middle, six blobs of dough
Not feeling anything. Then I woke up
Sweating with pain: no baby, nothing but darkness
Ticking with clocks, dripping with water, and blood
From clots of cottonwool sopping through my night-dress.
It was me in pain: and I'd thought my baby was
That never lived perhaps to feel a pain.
I felt relaxed, free, till the pain began.
It wasn't bad at first: just aching rubbing
From an internal graze: but it was agony
Like ripping bandages from the middle of my guts
When the plugs came out. It became routine.
Each morning, screens: and forceps picking at me,
Dismembering the corpse in penny numbers.
That last day was the worst. Like having the curse
Worse than when it's worst. I was having a baby
Born in bits. I could recognize it then:
Solid: not blood: I could see cells and things.
For two months since I've kept on wondering
Did it all come out? They said I'd take
A while to adjust to it, but I know for sure
It might be growing again from one bit left,
A resurrected monster, like a giant lizard
Sprung from a tadpole, gathering itself for revenge
On me and its father. This last half-hour
I've started noticing the Virgin Mary
Above the altar. Suppose she'd not believed

35

She was to be Christ's mother, taken precautions,
Aborted Him. Would anyone have blamed her
For not being taken in by wishful visions?
She was, though. She believed what she was told
And the child was born that God was Father to,
Planted by the angel. Listen, now: suppose
I was the victim of an angel, too,
One with powerful fins and the ability to live
Between these pink doors for days without weakening
Or dropping his wand. Only two people would know
If Christ came back I might have murdered Him
And you'd be one of them. You've said on Sundays
We're punished for our sins. What could mine be
For crucifying someone in my womb?

Report to the Director

I'd say their marble cubicles were a shade
Too small for the taller men, but they all appeared
To be standing at ease. Oh the usual postures – hands
In their pockets, hands on their hips, hands on the wall.
A few touched themselves. A few were saying prayers
Perhaps. I expect a few were feeling the cold
From that bare cement floor in those bedroom slippers.
I did, in my shoes; but still, I suppose one allows
A little latitude in the provinces. No money
To do it all in style. However, it worked
And we did get going. One man was reluctant
To cooperate about buttons – a big fellow
With a lot of weight to throw around: it's always

Annoying that sort of thing: a nasty business
It can be on those tiles. So we gave a hand,
Igor and I. The locals didn't mind,
They rarely do. From there it was plain sailing
To the main business. The five attendants came
All according to the book, well-turned-out men
In their new aprons, with the usual hoses, and a good
Flexible pump. (I gave them marks for that. You know
There's a lot of friction on those grids if they scuffle
When you fit the neck-plates.
It might be worthwhile specifying cable,
Steel-strapped stuff; it would save in the long run.)
Fortunately, we didn't need it: they were all so docile,
Queued and shuffled out with no trouble at all.
Though the line-up was tricky – they'd done the count wrong
So we had to use the shoe-horn on a couple.
But after that it was fine: taps on,
Mask fitted, the legs well held, the right grip
And a nice simple injection – I always think
Those gas cylinders are all wrong. The infusion
Was one of the smoothest I've seen. Evacuation
Very decent. An infinity of freshness
In a little diffusion of bitter carbolic. Rather sweet.
It took about fifteen minutes to get the stories,
And not much mess: they had to scrub the channel
To clear some vomit, otherwise all OK.
No frills: but at least the operation was completed
With all proper precautions, the doors closed,
The men screened: and, oh yes, the windows open
To clean the air. I doubt if anyone smelled
A rat in the whole building, or heard as much
As a squeak from a plimsoll. They moved like professionals
From start to finish. I'd say it was all good work.
They certainly do things with the minimum fuss.
I'd recommend we exonerate the whole depot.

Early Warning

Lord god of wings, forgive this hand
That stole from thee. These holy bones
Where thy long shadow ran I give
Thee back, repentant. From thy dead
Steel bird's ripped belly I and four
Doomed ice-men took them out, eight hands

Fouling thy sacred felled limbs. Two
Dropped bones I stooped and kicked. Forgive
Me, god. I never knew thy bones,
Delivered from the ice, could rise
And kill four men. I thought thou wast
Mortal as I. Thy lofty skull,

Smoothed by the Greenland wind, I stole
With my scarred hands. I thought last night
That whale-fat poured in thy round eyes
Would staunch the wind. If my hut stands
And others fell, no other cause
I seek for that. So when at dawn

Four ice-men died, burnt-up by thy
Bones' wrath, I thought: this jealous god's
Enduring skull, strong thigh-bone, I
Must give back safe, wise helps, sure harms
For cruel men. Forgive me, god,
For what I did. Those men thou burned

With inward hell that made them twist
In wrangling heaps were faithless. I
Repent my sin. If I should carve
A cross for thee, draped with a fish

Nailed through its hanging tail, wouldst thou
Dismiss this pain? I feel it come

Below the eyes, inside my head,
As they all said it came. Forgive
My theft. I give thee back thy skull,
Thy scalding thigh-bone, god. Thou shalt
Own all I have, my hut, my wife,
My friendly pack of dogs, if thou

Wilt only tell why these green scars
Ache in my cheeks; why this grey mould
Forms on my herring pail; why this
Right hand that touched thy head shrinks up;
And why this living fish I touched
Writhes on that plank, spoiled food for gulls?

Ash

So it was true. Elastic air could fill
    In a trice with particles
  And clapped earth give no warning. Ill
    With rage, they swallowed pills,
Floundered to hide-outs. Over the hogback southern hills

  A giant sifter shook black sugar. Bleeps
    On the tele-screen spelled SLEEP
  IT THROUGH. Eyes glued on sky-fed slag-heaps
    Peppering soot, watched sheep
Whose wool stank acrid stick at stiles no legs could leap.

The crushed air gently settled. In a slow
    Powdering like a crow's
  Wing mouldering, a thin tar snow
    Assembled, staining toes
Of barefoot children dug in sand it cast no shadows

  In but mingled with. What fitter night
    For prophesying flights
  Of rooks? In entrails needles might
    Probe omens. Grilled in tights,
A Creole whore screamed giving birth. Her brat's paired whites

  Shone like burnt coals. A Negro steeplejack
    Nine floors up welding cracks
  In scaffolding shrivelled on a rack
    Of poisoned iron. Packs
Of wolves burned. Chessboard queens in stained teak spat like
                        sacks

  Of roasted chestnuts on a grated fire
    Of sulphur. A church choir's
  Top alto charred. His Chrysler tyre
    Made licorice. The spire's
Incinerating copper boiled a bat. *Esquires*

  Where clutching fingers curled, shrank into what
    Crumbled like bad flour, blots
  Of putrefying matter, hot
    As frying kidneys. Shots
Of iced Scotch would have cooled one soldier's nerve-ends.
                        Dots

  And dashes flustered angry dials. Done
    Steaks grilled. Not everyone's
  Plop-footed warden, won

From melting wax, brought guns
To fortify stuffed cellars. When one came, few suns,

Rotting the bricked fumes, twisted through taut sashes
To explore a livid gash
Of wounded air where crackling lashes
Writhed. More times that rash
Of acid yellow faltered. What was left was ash.

The God of Love

The musk-ox is accustomed to near-Arctic conditions.
When danger threatens, these beasts cluster together to
form a defensive wall or a 'porcupine' with the calves in
the middle.

Dr Wolfgang Engelhardt,
Survival of the Free

I found them between far hills, by a frozen lake,
On a patch of bare ground. They were grouped
In a solid ring, like an ark of horn. And around
Them circled, slowly closing in,
Their tongues lolling, their ears flattened against the wind,

A whirlpool of wolves. As I breathed, one fragment of bone
and
Muscle detached itself from the mass and
Plunged. The pad of the pack slackened, as if
A brooch had been loosened. But when the bull
Returned to the herd, the revolving collar was tighter. And
only

41

The windward owl, uplifted on white wings
   In the glass of air, alert for her young,
Soared high enough to look into the cleared centre
   And grasp the cause. To the slow brain
Of each beast by the frozen lake what lay in the cradle of their
      crowned

Heads of horn was a sort of god-head. Its brows
   Nudged when the ark was formed. Its need
Was a delicate womb away from the iron collar
   Of death, a cave in the ring of horn
Their encircling flesh had backed with fur. That the collar of
      death

Was the bone of their own skulls: that a softer womb
   Would open between far hills in a plunge
Of bunched muscles: and that their immortal calf lay
   Dead on the snow with its horns dug into
The ice for grass: they neither saw nor felt. And yet if

That hill of fur could split and run – like a river
   Of ice in thaw, like a broken grave –
It would crack across the icy crust of withdrawn
   Sustenance and the rigid circle
Of death be shivered: the fed herd would entail its under-fur

On the swell of a soft hill and the future be sown
   On grass, I thought. But the herd fell
By the bank of the lake on the plain, and the pack closed,
   And the ice remained. And I saw that the god
In their ark of horn was a god of love, who made them die.

'The Spider's Nest

Was clenched on a fly's carcase like a golden
Fist which exploded into an abacus
Of excited beads at the prick of my quill'

Is one verse. 'This morning I arranged about
A hundred things with legs on invisible
Wires to dance attendance' is another. To

Be crippled and have such tensed will subdued by
A feather pleases. On a wheeled bed or an
Orbed web life rakes old sores over with my (or

Some other) tough hand. The feather of death in
One's bowels tickles the triumph out of such
Teasing of puissance. Day after day to lie

Here watching the sun skate in the sky, wanting
Death but unable to move except enough
To kill wasps with a book or annoy spiders,

Is something. After all, success in drowning
Ants in vermouth requires only time and I
Collect it like dust. Snakes come. Visitors with

French sonnets. Minestrone for supper. Floods
In May. If Stock insists on a third verse I
Suggest 'a few hesitated between the

Abrupt brink of air and the known centre of
A gauze mesh where their inherited fly lay
Spread out to be eaten' but I'm not keen on

43

A fourth verse. To leave great themes unfinished is
Perhaps the most satisfying exercise
Of power. Describing their look of being

The armour of a god left hanging over-
night in a skein of frost can be decently
Left to Vernon. Sleep comes. And with it my snails.

Florence, 1885, *Eugene Lee-Hamilton*

The Absentees

When Egil Skallagrimsson
Choked Grim's thralls to death at the
Age of eighty though quite blind
The astonished ravens by
The bog were certainly not

You and I. We should hardly
Have stood the spectacle. And
At Bosworth Field when Richard
The Third fell in the thickest
Press of his enemies those

Vultures hovering in the
Black sky were some other glum
Couple. We had better things
To do. Did Gabriele
D'Annunzio observe a

Brace of eagles change into

Pigeons above the fateful
Piave? Those mutable
Birds were perhaps Paola
And Francesca, not you and

I. We were too busy in
Other spheres. Carina, why
Do you worry that we shall
Not be there when the first ape
Steps onto the moon in a

Grey silk hat? I remember
Nothing about the nineteen
Twenties except that I must
Have wet my nappy. The sun
Turns. And your lips invite me.

Court Gossip

Despite the College of Physicians
Who claim much can be done, I believe
That a decent prudence would make plans
    For the end of the affair.

They prescribe books: a house in Leyden:
A boy to stoke the furnace. Without
Fail it will all help. In the end, though,
    We shall have to wind things up

With black-edged cards. The old gentleman

Is deranged. For the composition
Of teasing minutes prolonged flogging
    With a quaint thong. Pad sofas

To accommodate that versatile
Negress. Egyptian massage. Full aid
For the nerves. But at what cost! The
    Exchequer shakes. One shies at

Roman orgies. A dish of truffles:
Coan wine: the ineptitude of
Slave women. It tots up. The flesh is
    Heir to a mort of torments

But not this. Bustles, hair-splittings – where
Does one draw the line between resigned
Acceptance and a mean carping? Spare
    The rod and spoil the child. I

Anticipate the kiss of Lesbos,
The 'shall we row, darling', the obscene
Albums. Where is His Royal Highness
    To rove next? A back-scratcher?

Wading with lung-fishes? Assume that
One hires this belly-organ. A sip
Of benedictine, a whiff – and, pish!
    To your leopard-skins, your oiled

Fig silks. I admire the Comtessa's
Alive sense of values. To be suave
In full ruin demands refinement.
    A black banquet is rumoured

For the death of 'a close friend': claret:

A burnt chop: Puerto Ricans in tight
Velvet: a scent of burnt wax. Assured
  Boredom for three footmen with

Primed snuffers. Weeping Pierrots. The tears
Running on black net. We inherit
The ash and olive stones. In a jar
  Of iced honey a ju-jube.

So it ends. The magnificent fails,
Troughed in fingerbowls. The inspired,
Wistful, Athenian faultlessness
  Of Ludwig! And this lecher!

The Wasp-Woman

after Ponge

I

She could only mate in the air. Her body,
  a little heavier than
a mosquito's, the wings light and small, beating,

hovered in a million cells. Each spent moment
  she seemed to quiver as if
pinned on a fly-paper or drowning in thick

honey. She moved as if trapped always at a
  point of crisis which made her
the danger she was. Like a taut string whose touch

47

burned or cut as it yielded its resonance,
   she hurt as she moved. From her
belly the rich beating came. On the skin of

plums her nails moved like a machine for plucking
   something out. If her clothes rasped
on the edge of a plate, or brushed a cup where

the dregs of sugar remained, you could feel the
   dark pull of the world's honey,
straining her muscles.

II

The electric tram moves

on its rails. There is something deaf in repose
   and loud into gear about
it too. It breaks at the waist as she did. Is

shrivelled by electricity like something
   fried. And if you touched her, she
pricked. No shock, the venomous vibration from

all her pores: but her body was softer, her
   flight wilder, more unforeseen,
more dangerous than the even run of a

thing on rails.

III

   She was one of those wheeled machines
  that at certain seasons ride
from farm to farm in the country, providing

refreshment. A little pump grinding on wings.
  Nobody knowing how she
maintained her internal state of a tense poise

or constructed what she was selling. Whose whole
  activity was inside,
a thing of mystery and presumed wisdom.

A cauldron of jam, sealed from the air, and yet
  soft. And the drum in the groin
causing her to see-saw, as she rose in flight.

IV

One must always classify what is known by
  a character which endures,
and by which one could recognize it. And so

with her it is that skin. Perhaps rightly. I
  know nothing of it, I could
never swear to it. And yet with that wasp it

was not so odd to describe her wings as *like
  membranes*. Not that they looked like
a dark hymen. It was for historical

reasons. The abstraction remains, trailing the
  hard truths of a thing once felt.
In the coils of the living science there lies

the stretched, gauzy, tendentious, appropriate
  word for a wasp-woman. There
is nothing more in this line.

V

What else can one

say? That she left her sting in the victim and
    succumbs to it? In war that
never pays. The elaborate touchiness –

from fear or from over-sensitivity –
    has already punished her.
She has no advantage in risking a new

enemy, would zig-zag to miss a friend. *I
    know my ways*, she would say, *if
I attach myself it can only provoke*

*a crisis. We are too far apart. If once
    I accepted the pulse of
your world, I should spend my life in it. So launch*

*me in my groove and go on in yours. In the
    sleep-walking, the internal
deadness. Forget about explaining things*. It

was then that the world gave her a little knock,
    and she dropped. I could only
crush her to death.

VI

(Or was it perhaps that she

was touchy because of what she carried? And
    this justified her rage: her
consciousness of its value?)

VII

And yet this fine

deadness which could destroy her (one blow, and she
   dropped) could also save her, or
at least prolong her life. That dark wasp was so

stupid (I don't mean to abuse her) that if
   you cut her in two parts, she
continued to live. She took two days to know

she was dead. Her heart just went on beating. It
   beat faster than before. And
surely this was the zenith of preventive

stupidity? Stupidity in the gut.

VIII

  Swarm: from exagmen: from *ex*
agire: to push out.

IX

Such thirst perhaps from

the slenderness of her waist. For the Greeks the
   brain was in the waist. And they
used the same word for both. If it was *sponge*, they

were right.

X

Why was it so? That of all creatures
the fiercest one was the sun's
colour? And why are beaten things always the

savagest?

XI

She thrust into flesh as others
delve into fruit. Would wrestle,
mouth, warp, corrupt it. With her elastic-smooth,

marmalade-black body would smash, pulp, erase
the integrity of flesh,
even alter its feel of being alive.

When a wasp bites at a fruit there is never
such love-loathing, such many-
legged, insectuous writhing. She worked like a

black chemical, a violent process of
decomposition, marring
the flesh to a mess of pulp, exhausting the

seed.

XII

Listen to the plum speaking. *When the sun
ejaculates his honey,*
it scorches my skin. If the brisk wasp works her

sting into me, it rips my guts.

XIII

And she was
always eager for the full
honey-bin. Her temples quivering, her skin

trembling, and then the butterflies in her crutch:
a sort of squirt for sucking
sweetness in.

XIV

First there was the furnace. And then

the half-charred wasp was born, hissing, terrible
and by no means a matter
of indifference to Men-kind, for they faced

in her burning elegance their abortive
hunger for speed and for closed
flight through air. And in mine I saw an earthed fire

whose wings gushed out in all directions, and on
unforeseen trajectories.
It burned as if on offensive missions from

a nest in the ground. Like an engine out of
control, sometimes it trembled
as though she were not the mistress of her own

destructiveness. So at first that fire spread in
the earth, crackling, fluttering:
and then when the wings were accomplished, the sexed

wings, the antennaed squadrons broke out on their
    deadly business into the
flesh, and their work began to be finished, I

mean, her crime.

            In her swarm of words, the abrupt
    waspishness. But wait. Was this
devised flutter in the trench any more than

the weak rebellion of a few seeds, outraged
    by their sower? It was their
own violence that first brought them into his

apron. No, go back. This was a fire whose wings
    gushed out in all directions,
and on unforeseen trajectories. And I

faced in her burned elegance my abortive
    hunger for speed and for closed
flight through air. Or must one look further. Here was

the natural world on the wing. Her cruel
    divisions preparing their
offensive against male tyranny. I bared

my forests for their sting. But already her
    banked animosity was
flowing away in random fury. . . .

A swarm

of mute wasps worked over the countryside: and
   my unprotected nerves were
worked over by her.

And then one knock, one sharp

gunshot. And she seemed (herself like a gunshot
   recovering her fallen
decisiveness) to hurl herself with all haste

on her certain death. No, not quite. Like a shot,
   but less direct. As if when
the bullets left the gun the air seduced them

into forgetting their first intention, their
   straight road, their bitterness. Or
as if an army were sent to occupy

the nerve centres of a key city, and, once
   inside the main gates, became
absorbed into the bright things in windows, and

visited the museums, and drank from the
   straws of the men sipping wine
at the sidewalk cafés.

XVIII

And like gun-shots the

little nibbling bites she had once taken out
  of a thing saved up: as a
wasp riddles an upright wall of wormeaten

wood.

XIX

Or you could call her the instrument of
  that world-honey I spoke of
earlier. I mean a pent sweetness, needling,

repeated, beginning feebly, but awkward
  to shake off, and then striking
clear, with alternating force and weakness, and

so on. As the crisp wasp might well be called the
  musical form of honey:
ringing, insistent, devouring and fragile.

XX

And so on. Perhaps one day there will be a
  critic. And he will REPROACH
me for so inserting into poetry

my importunate, irritating and dead
  wasp-woman. And will DENOUNCE
the seductive appeal of her, and the way

she appears in so many sharp pieces, and
  zig-zags. And will be DISTURBED
at her lack of smooth coordination, and

piquancy without depth (though not without some
    danger) and all that. And will
treat my wasp-woman with all the abuse and

puzzlement she so richly deserves. I shall
    not worry, dear reader. The
harm was first done by a French poet in prose.

The Disciple

    I wore a black band. I thought
    They would crucify Him in jail. The
Word broke from His agony in the cells. I
    Awoke transfigured by incarnate
    Will. When He walked out alive I knew
That He was our Saviour. I remember His
    Burned face sharp in a nimbus
Of blurred light against the taut flags when He spoke

    To our massed lifted hands at
    The Rally. I knelt chilled by the bare
Marble before the fed flame for His dead
    Martyrs. I knew in my caught heart we
    Must all repeat His suffering. I
Wept the oath. I was dedicated to the
    Stern commitments of a snapped
Order. I swore to purify my blood of

    Evil. I accepted the
    Fires of hell on earth. Each uniform

I wore was as my flesh. Its coarse fibres were
  Burned by Evil, scraped bare of dust of
  Evil, encrusted with excrement
Of Evil. I breathed Evil in the stench of
    The bean soup we drank, the bags
Of charcoal I unheaped for the furnaces,

    The pit of my soul. When I
  Raked the ovens or even touched a
Spade I felt sick. I vomited when I saw
  The pyramid of their bodies for
  The first time. When a crying child stretched
Out her arms to me I was moved to sweep her
    Clear of the doors. I was not
A strong-willed man. I fought to do the hard thing

    Well but the Evil within
  Me fought back. I lay awake hearing
Them scream. I committed the sin of pity
  For Evil every time I touched
  Their brittle limbs. In my dreams I was
Watching my infant sister crawled on by stick
    Insects with human faces.
Gas was like incense: it drowned corruption. In

    The wind or in cylinders
  To be raised and used it became a
Presence more real than His. Above my bed
  His tense eyes looked down while I slept and
  Forgave or condemned. His enormous
Words on the air proved that He still existed
    And surely cared: but I held
A scarred ikon close to my heart which showed Him

    Massacred in the streets by

58

The Blood of Evil. I walked in the
Foul heresy of admiring His weakness
   More than His rise to power: but I
   Groped my way back. The laceration
Of conscience began to ease. And the toil of
      Confronting the Evil in
Others began to confront the Evil in

      Me. I was helped. I confessed
   My doubts. I endured the controlling
Speech and hands of those more sure in their faith than
   I. And by Grace I recovered my
   Sanity and was purified in
Body and spirit. Behind a locked door in
      A blaze of light on a plain
Slate floor my schism was healed by the salt of

      Fear. I have no stain left to
   Scour. I cut into your wire a saved
Man. I am freed from sin by the mechanism
   Of holy justice. I heard of His
   Death as if the meaning of Life had
Been for a moment suspended but felt no
      Grief. I have shed my heavy
Cross and abide my end in peace of spirit.

Mother Superior

Sisters, it will be necessary
To prepare a cool retreat. See to
It that several basins are filled
Nightly with fresh water and placed there.
Take care that food for a long stay be

Provided in sealed jars. I know of
No way to protect an outer room
From the light but some must be tried. Let
The walls be made thick to keep out the
Heat. Before the Annunciation

Our Lord exacts no other service.
It may seem prudent to wear a wool
Robe at all times and to bow down when
The Word comes. Remember the parable
Of the Virgins and pray for all the

Unpremeditating. 'The brides of
Our Lord in their burrows' may not be
A flattering title but the known
Future lies in the wombs of prepared
Rabbits. To bear a pure strain with no

Care for the word's corruption requires
Courage, sisters. Creating a safe
Place for the incarnation of what
One can scarcely imagine without
Madness might seem a demeaning task.

In the Order of Resurrection
Of which you are acolytes there is

No more noble service. Remember
The Code. Your duty is not to the
Sick but to the unborn. Perform it.

The Son

Her body was all stones. She lay
In the stones like a glass marble. There was
        No moisture in her. There
Was only the dry spleen and the liver
    Gone hard as pumice stone. I closed

Her eyes. I saw a sole once on
A block of green marble. It was flung straight
        From the living brine, its
Pupils were bright with a strange heat. I watched
    A cat eat it alive. When I

Touched her cheek, the light failed. When I
Moved my open hand on her lips, there was
        No life there. She smelled of
The cheap soap we had washed her in. I saw
    The black hollows below her eyes

Where desire swam. I called her name
In the dark, but no-one answered. There was
        Only the sap rising.
I thought of the clotted mercury in
    The broken thermometer of

Her body. It rose again in
My head to a silver column, a sword
　　　Of blood in the sun. I
Held to its cross of fire in a dream of
　　Climbing. I swam in the air: my

Wings were extended into the
Night. I was borne above the clouds: I flew
　　　At increasing speeds, to
Increasing altitudes. There was only
　　The sun above me. I *was* the

Sun. The world was my mother, I
Spread my wings to protect her growth. She broke
　　　Into wheat and apples
Beneath my rain. I came with my fire to
　　The sea, to the earth from the air,

To the broken ground with my fresh
Seed. I lay on her cold breast, inhaling
　　　The scent of iris and
Daffodils. There was nothing more to be
　　Settled. I thought of her dying

Words, how butter would scarcely melt
In her mouth. I heard a wheel squeak and the
　　　Drip of water. I touched
The cold rail and the covering sheet. Your
　　Light shone in my eyes. Forgive me.

The Killing

In a wooden room, surrounded by lights and
    Faces, the place where death had
Come to its sharpest point was exposed. In a
    Clear shell they examined the
    Needle of death. How many
  Million deaths were concentrated in

A single centre! The compass of death was
    Lifted, detached and broken,
Taken and burned. The seed of death lay in the
    Hold. Without disturbance or
    Ceremony they sealed it
  In foil. The ship stirred at the quay. The

Pilot was ready. A long shadow slanted
    On the harbour water. The
Fin bearing the ignorant crew on their brief
    Journey cut through the air. Three
    Furlongs out at sea the
  Strike of the engine fell. The screws turned

At ease on the rim of the world. The hour had
    Come. The action was taken.
The doors opened. And the ash went out to sea
    Borne with the moon on the tide
    Away from the shore towards the
  Open water. The shell rocked on the

Livid waves. The captain washed his hands in the
    Salt to cleanse the illusion
Of blood. The light casket lay on the soaked planks
    Emptied of all it held. And

A pale fish that used to leap
For a fly or a grub to the bare

Trees and then sink back to the living water
        Forgot the way: and died in
The dry branches. The baked island was crusted
        With the blue eggs of terns from
        Which no soft wings would ever
    Break to fly in the sun. And the raw

Turtle crawled inland instead of towards the
        Sea, believing the parched soil
Would change to sand again. They thought the killing
        Was over: but the needle
        Had run wild in the shell. The
    Poison was in the salt current of

The world. Let no Jew or Gentile believe that
        The fly in the brain of the
Bald man adjusting his earphones annuls his
        Own nature; nor pity the
        Man imprisoned for stealing
    Fire from heaven. He, too, is guilty.

A True Story

When the British Association
For the Advancement of Science held
Its Annual Meeting one year in
        East Anglia no-one could

Think what to feed them on. It appeared
From previous experience in
County Durham that members consumed
    An enormous quantity

Of sandwiches. How were the hundreds
Of visiting scientists to be
Fed? The problem was finally solved
    By the inspiration of

A Norfolk poacher who suggested
At a public meeting in the Town
Hall at Norwich the employment of
    Their local pest the Coypu

Rat. He claimed that between two layers
Of freshly cut bread a thick slice of
Coypu tasted quite delicious. And
    It proved so. At any rate

The sandwiches were bought and eaten
In extraordinarily large
Numbers. The plain bread seemed to set off
    The unusual taste of

The dead rodent. Indeed a group of
Younger men from the Biology
Section dissected the furry beasts
    With a view to assessing

Just why. Altogether it was 'a
Great success for the quality of
Willingness to experiment' as
    The Countryman aptly said.

Missile Commander

I guess to be spending one's time
spitting cherry-stones into iced
water (counting how many float
and how many sink) might not seem

a task of much high reward for
an ex-Colonel of Infantry
on a missile site. No, sir. But
do you know what better way there

is of keeping a sound fit mind
in a guaranteed, processed-steel,
crap-proof bunker protected from
any shit but a direct hit

on Texas? I can tell you there's
a clear blue eye and a fine stiff
upper lip needed for spitting
cherry-stones. Yes, sir. Do you know

that in twelve days, allowing one
spit at dinner one spit at lunch
per day, the current score (just for
the record) is *nearly seven*

*hundred and thirty-three up for one
hundred and eighty-two down?* I
guess in Georgia those red bastards
are pushing around one sixty-

five now. According to our checked
latest reports they sure are hard

on our heels. So if you'll excuse
my rudeness I'll just stick with my

conviction we can keep our nose
ahead of those Russkies only
through constant vigilance by our
little bowl of white cherry-stones.

The Crab-Apple Crisis

for Martin Bell

To make this study concrete I have devised a ladder – a metaphorical
ladder – which indicates that there are many continuous paths between
a low-level crisis and an all-out war.

Herman Kahn 'On Escalation'

LEVEL 1: COLD WAR
    RUNG 1: OSTENSIBLE CRISIS

Is that you, Barnes? Now see here, friend. From
where I am I can see your boy quite
clearly soft-shoeing along towards
my crab-apple tree. And I want you

to know I can't take that.

RUNG 2: POLITICAL, ECONOMIC AND DIPLOMATIC GESTURES

If you don't
wipe that smile off your face, I warn you

I shall turn up the screw of my frog
transistor above the whirr of your

lawn-mower.

RUNG 3: SOLEMN AND FORMAL DECLARATIONS

Now I don't want to sound
unreasonable but if that boy
keeps on codding round my apple tree
I shall have to give serious thought

to taking my belt to him.

LEVEL II: DON'T ROCK THE BOAT
RUNG 4: HARDENING OF POSITIONS

I thought
you ought to know that I've let the Crows
walk their Doberman through my stack of
bean canes behind your chrysanthemum

bed.

RUNG 5: SHOW OF FORCE

You might like a look at how my
boy John handles his catapult. At
nineteen yards he can hit your green-house
pushing four times out of five.

RUNG 6: SIGNIFICANT MOBILIZATION

I've asked

the wife to call the boy in for his
coffee, get him to look out a good
supply of small stones.

RUNG 7: 'LEGAL' HARASSMENT

                    Sure fire my lawn
spray is soaking your picnic tea-cloth

but I can't be responsible for
how those small drops fall, now can I?

RUNG 8: HARASSING ACTS OF VIOLENCE

                              Your
kitten will get a worse clip on her
left ear if she come any nearer

to my rose-bushes, mam.

RUNG 9: DRAMATIC MILITARY CONFRONTATIONS

                    Now see here,
sonny, I can see you pretty damn
clearly up here. If you come one step
nearer to that crab-apple tree you'll

get a taste of this strap across your
back.

LEVEL III: NUCLEAR WAR IS UNTHINKABLE
RUNG 10: PROVOCATIVE DIPLOMATIC BREAK

I'm not going to waste my time
gabbing to you any longer, Barnes:
I'm taking this telephone off the

hook.

RUNG 11: ALL IS READY STATUS

Margery, bring that new belt of
mine out on the terrace, would you? I
want these crazy coons to see we mean
business.

RUNG 12: LARGE CONVENTIONAL WAR

Take that, you lousy kraut. My

pop says you're to leave our crab-apple
tree alone. Ouch! Ow! I'll screw you for
that.

RUNG 13: LARGE COMPOUND ESCALATION

OK, you've asked for it. The Crows'
dog is coming into your lilac

bushes.

RUNG 14: DECLARATION OF LIMITED CONVENTIONAL WAR

Barnes. Can you hear me through this
loud-hailer? OK. Well, look. I have
no intention of being the first
to use stones. But I will if you do.

Apart from this I won't let the dog
go beyond your chrysanthemum bed
unless your son actually starts
to climb the tree.

RUNG 15: BARELY NUCLEAR WAR

                    Why, no. I never

told the boy to throw a stone. It was
an accident, man.

RUNG 16: NUCLEAR ULTIMATUM

                    Now see here. Why
have you wheeled your baby into the
toolshed? We've not thrown stones.

RUNG 17: LIMITED EVACUATION

                              Honey. I

don't want to worry you but their two
girls have gone round to the Jones's.

RUNG 18: SPECTACULAR SHOW OF FORCE

                              John.
Throw a big stone over the tree, would
you: but make sure you throw wide.

RUNG 19: JUSTIFIABLE ATTACK

                              So we

threw a stone at the boy. Because he
put his foot on the tree. I warned you
now, Barnes.

RUNG 20: PEACEFUL WORLD-WIDE EMBARGO OR BLOCKADE

          Listen, Billy, and you too
Marianne, we've got to teach this cod

a lesson. I'm asking your help in
refusing to take their kids in, or
give them any rights of way, or lend
them any missiles until this is

over.

LEVEL IV: NO NUCLEAR USE
RUNG 21: LOCAL NUCLEAR WAR

          John. Give him a small fistful
of bricks. Make sure you hit him, but not
enough to hurt.

RUNG 22: DECLARATION OF LIMITED NUCLEAR WAR

                    Hello there, Barnes. Now
get this, man. I propose to go on

throwing stones as long as your boy is
anywhere near my tree. Now I can
see you may start throwing stones back and
I want you to know that we'll take that

without going for your wife or your
windows unless you go for ours.

RUNG 23: LOCAL NUCLEAR WAR – MILITARY

                              We
propose to go on confining our
stone-throwing to your boy beside our

tree: but we're going to let him have
it with all the stones we've got.

RUNG 24: EVACUATION OF CITIES – ABOUT 70 PER CENT

                              Sweetie.
Margery. Would you take Peter and
Berenice round to the Switherings?

Things are getting pretty ugly.

LEVEL V: CENTRAL SANCTUARY
RUNG 25: DEMONSTRATION ATTACK ON ZONE OF INTERIOR

                        We'll
start on his cabbage plot with a strike
of bricks and slates. He'll soon see what we
could do if we really let our hands

slip.

RUNG 26: ATTACK ON MILITARY TARGETS

        You bastards. Sneak in and smash our
crazy paving, would you?

RUNG 27: EXEMPLARY ATTACKS AGAINST PROPERTY

                    We'll go for
their kitchen windows first. Then put a
brace of slates through the skylight.

RUNG 28: ATTACKS ON POPULATION

                        OK.

Unless they pull out, chuck a stone or
two into the baby's pram in the
shed.

RUNG 29: COMPLETE EVACUATION – 95 PER CENT

They've cleared the whole family, eh,
baby and all. Just Barnes and the boy

left. Best get your mom to go round to
the Switherings.

RUNG 30: RECIPROCAL REPRISALS

Well, if they smash the
bay window we'll take our spunk out on
the conservatory.

LEVEL VI: CENTRAL WAR
RUNG 31: FORMAL DECLARATION OF GENERAL WAR

Now listen,

Barnes. From now on in we're going all
out against you – windows, flowers, the
lot. There's no hauling off now without
a formal crawling-down.

RUNG 32: SLOW-MOTION COUNTER-FORCE WAR

We're settling

in for a long strong pull, Johnny. We'd
better try and crack their stone stores one
at a time. Pinch the bricks, plaster the
flowers out and smash every last

particle of glass they've got.

74

RUNG 33: CONSTRAINED REDUCTION

>   We'll have
> to crack that boy's throwing arm with a
> paving stone. Just the arm, mind. I don't
> want him killed or maimed for life.

RUNG 34: CONSTRAINED DISARMING ATTACK

>   Right, son.

> We'll break the boy's legs with a strike of
> bricks. If that fails it may have to come
> to his head next.

RUNG 35: COUNTER-FORCE WITH AVOIDANCE

>   There's nothing else for
> it. We'll have to start on the other

> two up at the Jones's. If the wife
> and the baby gets it, too, it can't
> be helped.

LEVEL VII: CITY TARGETING
RUNG 36: COUNTER-CITY WAR

>   So it's come to the crunch. His
> Maggie against my Margery. The

> kids against the kids.

RUNG 37: CIVILIAN DEVASTATION

>   We can't afford
> holds barred any more. I'm going all
> out with the slates, tools, bricks, the whole damn
> shooting match.

All right, Barnes. This is it.

Get out the hammer, son: we need our
own walls now. I don't care if the whole
block comes down. I'll get that maniac
if it's the last thing I – Christ. O, Christ.

Drop

Sky was the white soil you
Grew in. When the fourth stick broke
    Into thistledown
At the crack of a whistle, streaked brown

From the crutch out with a crust
Of fear it was like an orgasm to
    Fork into air.
I could see why they'd nicked that nylon

Rip cord 'the release'. We
Spread like a leprosy on their clean
    Sun to the wogs. You
Could see their screwed heads grow up

Like dry coal we'd got
To clap a match to. Christ it was good
    To feel the sick
Flap of the envelope in the wind:

Like galloping under a stallion's
Belly. Half of Africa flushed
      Out and cocked
Up: you could piss in its eye. You could want to

  Scream the Marseillaise like a
Hymn. And then it was all gone.
      Splum. You were sinking
In a hot bog you'd never wrench

  Clear of alive. Soaked,
Vomiting, jelly-marrowed, afraid
      To spit. No life
Left but that leg-breaking drop on a

  Split stockade where they'd have your
Genitals off. You were strung up like Jesus
      Christ in the strings
Of your own carriage: lynched by the Kosher

  Sluts who'd packed your chute.
It couldn't work. You were on your own.
      The stick had died
In the screws or never dropped. When the ground

  Slammed you at eighteen feet
Per second you were out skedaddling for the first
      Tree with your harness
Cut: the sten jammed whore-

  hot yammering out of your
Groin. You were implementing the drill
      Balls: it was flog
On till you blacked out dead.

Scissor-Man

I am dangerous
  in a crisis
with sharp legs and a screw

  in my genitals. I slice
bacon-rind for a living. At nights I
  lie dried

under the draining-board, dreaming
  of Nutcrackers
and the Carrot-grater. If I should

  catch him rubbing
those tin nipples of hers
  in the bread-bin

(God rust his pivot!) so much for
  secrecy. I'd have his
washer off. And

  then what? It scarcely pays
to be 'Made In Hamburg'. Even
  our little salt-spoon

can sound snooty
  with an E.P.N.S. under
his armpit. Even the pie-server

  who needs re-dipping. In sixteen
stainless years dividing
  chippolata-links I

am still denied
   a place in the sink unit. And
you can imagine

   what pairing-off is possible
with a wriggle of cork-screws
   in an open knife-box. So I

keep my legs
   crossed. I never cut up
rough. I lie with care

   in a world where a squint leg
could be fatal. I sleep like a weapon
   with a yen for a pierced ear.

The Viking

He doesn't even have strength left to wind his watch
When he wakes up. I can shake sleep out of my body
Like the drops of a shower. I lick his foot
With my rasping tongue, pretending to wash him.

Aw, he says, weakly, rubbing my ear.
He tastes of nothing to me. I can wash and drink
With the same organ, as he can perhaps fornicate
And make water, without comparisons. He needs wool
   blankets

To warm his hollow torso. Even in winter
I curl in the wind and sleep strongly without aids.

I look with a green eye on all copulations,
Doctored by his white vet: but I can be swift

And kill birds on the branch of the mock-orange tree
With a wild leap. Can he? I am alive
Risen from the salt brine and the long barrows
Coiled in a cat's springs. He hasn't even died.

Afterlife

I

I can see in the dark but my eyes
  look much too big
in the soup-tins. I am always
  amazed to see myself.

II

In my wire bowl I can scarcely
  arrange my tail
without bringing a pound of strawberry
  jam on my back. I am too athletic.

III

It helps to be decently tricked out
  with a pair of hands
you could hide in a watch-
  case, of course. I have to spend

so much time eating
to keep warm.

IV

Having gnawed through their Japanese house
    I no longer investigate
Rice Crispies for signs
    of tops. I am all saliva.

V

The eccentric pleasures of arching at high
    speeds over quite
unbelievably large tracts
    of space are palling.

As are the delights
of messy activities amid flour.

VI

I have not yet approached the arctic
    regions of my world flowing
with milk and honey. Why risk
    such excoriating cold

for wrapped meat?

VII

I could live on the shelves for
    years without touching the ground.
There might be enough cauliflower
    for the rest of my life.

Bedtime Story

Long long ago when the world was a wild place
Planted with bushes and peopled by apes, our
Mission Brigade was at work in the jungle.
    Hard by the Congo

Once, when a foraging detail was active
Scouting for green-fly, it came on a grey man, the
Last living man, in the branch of a baobab
    Stalking a monkey.

Earlier men had disposed of, for pleasure,
Creatures whose names we scarcely remember –
Zebra, rhinoceros, elephants, wart-hog,
    Lion, rats, deer. But

After the wars had extinguished the cities
Only the wild ones were left, half-naked
Near the Equator: and here was the last one,
    Starved for a monkey.

By then the Mission Brigade had encountered
Hundreds of such men: and their procedure,
History tells us, was only to feed them:
    Find them and feed them;

Those were the orders. And this was the last one.
Nobody knew that he was, but he was. Mud
Caked on his flat grey flanks. He was crouched, half-
    armed with a shaved spear

Glinting beneath broad leaves. When their jaws cut
Swathes through the bark and he saw fine teeth shine,

Round eyes roll round and forked arms waver
    Huge as the rough trunks

Over his head, he was frightened. Our workers
Marched through the Congo before he was born, but
This was the first time perhaps that he'd seen one.
    Staring in hot still

Silence, he crouched there: then jumped. With a long swing
Down from his branch, he had angled his spear too
Quickly, before they could hold him, and hurled it
    Hard at the soldier

Leading the detail. How could he know Queen's
Orders were only to help him? The soldier
Winced when the tipped spear pricked him. Unsheathing his
    Sting was a reflex.

Later the Queen was informed. There were no more
Men. An impetuous soldier had killed off,
Purely by chance, the penultimate primate.
    When she was certain,

Squadrons of workers were fanned through the Congo
Detailed to bring back the man's picked bones to be
Sealed in the archives in amber. I'm quite sure
    Nobody found them

After the most industrious search, though.
Where had the bones gone? Over the earth, dear,
Ground by the teeth of the termites, blown by the
    Wind, like the dodo's.

Owl

is my favourite. Who flies
like a nothing through the night,
who-whoing. Is a feather
duster in leafy corners ring-a-rosy-ing
boles of mice. Twice

you hear him call. Who
is he looking for? You hear
him hoovering over the floor
of the wood. O would you be gold
rings in the driving skull

if you could? Hooded and
vulnerable by the winter suns
owl looks. Is the grain of bark
in the dark. Round beaks are at
work in the pellety nest,

resting. Owl is an eye
in the barn. For a hole
in the trunk owl's blood
is to blame. Black talons in the
petrified fur! Cold walnut hands

on the case of the brain! In the reign
of the chicken owl comes like
a god. Is a goad in
the rain to the pink eyes,
dripping. For a meal in the day

flew, killed, on the moor. Six
mouths are the seed of his

arc in the season. Torn meat
from the sky. Owl lives
by the claws of his brain. On the branch

in the sever of the hand's
twigs owl is a backward look.
Flown wind in the skin. Fine
rain in the bones. Owl breaks
like the day. Am an owl, am an owl.

Noah's Journey

I

The Building of the Ark

   oak

     is the keel. He is agèd and
gnarl-faced. See, he is here
with his acorns and edged leaves.
Off with his bark and his big
roots. Oak is an old friend.
Lays down his light beams, dips
them in warm tar: submits to
a varnish on one side. Is all
washed and ready for when storm comes.

     I am well-grained. I lie flat,
     hold off the water and float on

the waves. Once grounded, I
wait for a sailing, alert in the sun.

pine

   is the mast. He is upright,
   smooth, straight and long-limbed.
   He moves like a ramrod,
   casting aside all his twigs and his
   branches. A few cones
   curling an eyebrow predict when the
   rain's due. Standing in place now,
   spun in a socket he sets like a
   maypole. An oiled bole of red wood.

     Screwed to the low deck, I
     rise to the cold stars. The sea waits,
     tossing a little. The black earth
     lingers to wave me a long farewell.

II

The Entry of the Animals

mouse

   comes first. You can find
   him in holes. Out of the steel
   trap he would take your cheese
   with a flip of his foot. But, phlung!
   down the hard cold hat comes and
   is off with his ears. Is it
   so, mouse? Out of your wooden
   house come, mouse, and answer me.
   There is work for your teeth in the ark.

     Noah, Noah, I dare not come

out. There are too many cats.
And I fear for my tail. I will
come for some Brie.

bat

flies next like a broken
umbrella. Are you there, blind
bat, in the wind and the dark?
You may squeak in the hold to
the spider in the beam. I will
mend your wing. There are sound-
proofed boards for your sensitive
ears. Come down, sharp bat, with
your wife, and be friends.

I am here all the time at
your hand. So quietly I flew
that you never knew. I am
warm in the pit of your arm, blind Noah.

rat

leaves a sinking ship. Wise
brown rat, is there blame in that?
If you have to leave the
ark you must oar your way out
with an ant and a ladybird
aloft on your snout. Rat, make a
ring, be a life-belt here.
And gnaw me a port-hole or two
to see through. That will keep you quiet.

Rough Noah, I will not. I prefer
a biscuit. And as for sinking,

why it doesn't bear thinking. I
will nip your ankle if you nag at me.

lynx

is my look-out. He can see
in the murk. Yellow falls the
fog but the perk-eared lynx
feels vigilant. On the branch of
the mast he is pinned by his
claws. Telescoped in muscle
waits lynx for the land. With
a leap he will land, be the
first one on Ararat. Eh, peaked lynx?

I am anxious to rest my eyes.
Keep me away from the dazzle of
the zebra and the dots of the
leopard. I will stare at the plain bear.

pig

will need guiding with this
boar board. He is heavy with
acorns. Incontinent pig!
Why did they send me a pig
so big? You must learn to
be slimmer from the wolf or
the hare. I will fit you in
below decks. But you must keep
still, and not overlay any beast.

I am usefully fat. I can
keep some warm. There is sure

88

> *to be ice. And I shan't*
> *need heat.*

bear

are you there? Why, you smell
of honey. You voracious small bear!
Why have you come with your paws all
sticky? Go down to the sink.
You must dance for your
supper, and it won't be sweets.
Coarse brown bread for omnivorous
bears. And a beaker of brine
if we have to keep washing you in drinking water.

> *I am sorry, Noah. But I grew*
> *quite faint. So I stopped by a hive*
> *for a rest and a meal.*
> *Let me give you a hug.*

tiger

is a stick along railings. Like a
ripple in a lake he has lodged
in your eye. Come, tiger, you
are here. Tensed sinews in the rain.
Stretch out on the poop. Glare
over the orb of the ocean and
frighten the hail. We are safe,
mewed up in our tub with a
tiger to care for us. Tiger, look fierce.

> *With a roar and a bounce I*
> *will tear up the clouds. Keep*
> *plenty of meat, though, for me. I will*
> *wait like a rug.*

89

crocodile

creeps out of the swamp with a
creak and a snap. He is made like a
bag. He can float for a day
without winking his eye. In the mud
of the bayou he has pondered the flood
and decided to miss it. So come in,
long crocodile, and crawl to your space.
You can help make logs. We shall soon
need a fire. Lie there, and snap.

> *I would snap with a will. I have*
> *toothache, though. Please, Noah, will you*
> *give me a pill. In a mouth like mine*
> *pain sprouts like a bush.*

rhinoceros

comes aboard like a boulder. He is
lapped in hard layers like a
hot-water tank. We must study
him hard to improve the ark's
lagging. What a load you are
for us, lily-eared rhinoceros! If
you were to jump we should
plump to the bottom. Stand here
on this stout plank. And have some hay.

> *I don't eat hay. I am*
> *sorry, I must say, to be such*
> *a burden. Will it help if I lift*
> *my little ox-pecker off?*

elephant

comes last in his loose grey skin. In
the sun you can see brown
hairs on his back. I am sure he
will help to haul the ark
along the flat canal to the flood
when the water has come. He is
not forgetful of all the food
he will need. Have you brought green
leaves, ant-like and prudent elephant?

Aye, aye, Noah, I have hauled
this tree. It will feed huge me
for a year. Is there space
in the barge?

whale

must swim by the side of
the ship. If I take a dip
I can ride safe back on his
broad black head. Whale is
the biggest, are you not,
vast whale? In a storm you
can shelter the ship from the
waves. I will feed you for this
with plenty of plankton.

I am partial to plankton. I will
swim by your side. Yes, I will swim
by the ark's hind rim
and soothe the poor beasts who are sick.

The Battle with the Elements

thunder

is the one who is blundering
about. I can hear him in the
sky like a lout in the attic.
Bricks he would hurl if he
had them. Bing. Bang. He is
round like a gong with a
big bronze face. Say boo to
a goose he would not were it
not for his flick-nosed cousin.

*Talk big, small man, while you
can. I will bash you. Just
give me a minute to blow up
my balloon. You wait.*

lightning

is another. Oh another
matter. Snears through the ether
like a spear. Shrip-shrivels
into shreds your elaborate
ladders. Is a daze on the
deck. Stiff blitz to the sheets.
Fit scissors for the ropes
of the bark's tossed body. In a fit
you are cracked, split, ruined.

*Nix, Noah, you exaggerate a
little. You're afloat. I can
see a green pug-dog awash in the stern,
but the fireworks are finished, I'm off to bed.*

rain

is the one who goes on. He is flung
pita-pata-pita-pata from a
tipped bowl of dry peas. Wet fur,
wet wood, wet wings, wet canvas: the
whole wide world is awash in a
sluice of beans. Rattle, rush.
Down comes the roof in a slush
of cold glass bits. Below decks
glum beasts peer out and steam dry slowly.

I pour on. Always in
motion, a flow in the air, I
slither to all points. And fill earth
top-full of water, of water, of water.

wind

is the last one. A wild thing,
over the flat sea, the smooth
sea, he wanders. Whistling a
thin tune, a high tune, a shrill tune,
whirling the waves to a white, whizzed,
whipped-cream. Zing, zing, zing: and the
ark like a roundabout rolls up and
down, up and down, in a frenzy.
Packed close like sardines, the poor beasts are
    all sick

I breathe on. Puffing my fat
cheeks, I fill the small ship's
sails: blow it towards sand,
send it to new shores.

grass

grows beyond rock. The fur
of the soaked earth. The sweet
green coat of the land we
must stand upon. Ho, there, grass.
Are you dry behind the ears after all
that rain? Are you ready
for my green-fly to clamber in
your hair? Make room for
my elephant to land on your hide.

Noah, you may safely land. I was the
first to dry. This is your
warm and expected haven. And
here is your long-lost dove and your raven.

When I Am Dead

I desire that my body be
properly clothed. In such things
as I may like at the time.

And in the pockets may there be
placed such things as I use at the time
as pen, camera, wallet, file.

And I desire to be laid on my side
face down: since I have bad dreams
if I lie on my back.

No one shall see my face when I die.

And beside me shall lie
my stone pig
with holes in his eyes.

And the coffin shall be as big as a crate.
No thin box
for the bones only.

Let there be room for a rat to come in.

And see that my cat, if I have one then,
shall have my liver.
He will like that.

And lay in food for
a week and a day:
chocolate, meat, beans, cheese.

And let all lie in
the wind and the rain.
And on the eighth day burn.

And the ash
scatter as the wind decides.
And the stone and metal be dug in the ground.

This is my will.

The Red Herring

after Cros

There was once a high wall, a bare wall. And
against this wall, there was a ladder,
a long ladder. And on the ground,
under the ladder, there was a red
herring. A dry red herring.

And then a man came along. And in his hands
(they were dirty hands) this man had
a heavy hammer, a long nail
(it was also a sharp nail) and
a ball of string. A thick ball of string.

All right. So the man climbed up
the ladder (right up to the top)
and knocked in the sharp nail:
spluk! Just like that.
Right on top of the wall. The bare wall.

Then he dropped the hammer. It dropped
right down to the ground. And onto the nail
he tied a piece of string, a long
piece of string, and onto the string
he tied the red herring. The dry red herring.

And let it drop. And then he climbed
down the ladder (right down
to the bottom), picked up the hammer
and also the ladder (which was pretty heavy)
and went off. A long way off.

And since then, that red herring, the dry
red herring on the end of the string, which is
quite a long piece, has been
very very slowly swinging and
swinging to a stop. A full stop.

I expect you wonder why I made
up this story, such a simple story. Well,
I did it just to annoy people.
Serious people. And perhaps also
to amuse children. Small children.

Fin du Globe

Rules

The game is best played with a dealer and four players who
are known as North, South, East and West. The pack consists
of fifty-two postcards and four *fin du globe* cards which should
be shuffled by the dealer before each reading. An approxi-
mately equal number of cards should be handed by the dealer
to each of the four players. These cards may be arranged in
any order provided they are kept face down until they are read.
Players must read the first card in their hand when called on
by the dealer who may call them in any order he chooses
provided the same player is not called on twice running. Each
hand is terminated by the first player who turns up and reads
out one of the four *fin du globe* cards. The game is best played
in three hands.

Seatoller *The Captain to Rodrigo*

It has rained every day. Indeed, the annual mean rainfall here is the highest in England. We can only get the photographs by bubble-car. I can hardly believe that Millicent is lonely, but keep the dogs leashed. I shall write later.

Bogotà *Courtelle to Sigmund*

In the hills they say there are Indians who believe in the myth of the Flood. We shall need their resolution. My love to Johnny. But don't do anything yet about the van Loon. The tide may turn.

Andritsaina *Nicholas Emery to Commander Singal*

I have just picked up the news from the South Gap on the Gabo transistor. We must act soon in the Cheddar Gorge. Despite the weather the temple was looking extremely sexy. I signed my name in the visitor's book in a thunderstorm. Klebben is drying out by the fire.

Samarkand *Rivers to Favorita*

The airship is well on its way to Afghanistan. In this climate the Captain should be over the Gulf by Sunday. The Casbah is alive with rumours. Why don't the Hussars advance in the Khyber? How far is Alaric from Moscow?

Karachi *Sigmund to the Captain*

I am feeling a little sick. Last night I discovered a copy of your book with a bullet-hole in the spine. The heat is certainly terrific. If the Chinese attack again, there is nothing for it but to cede the Nagas. Without machine guns we are nothing.

Inishboffin *Raymond Allister to Elvira Norman*

There is no hope. Verne is aware of the stresses, but what can he do? If only we had artillery. The North Col is a possible route, as you say. But I think the Bishop should go in first.

Algiers *Philippa to Mrs Noakes*

This morning I found a scarab inside a packet of crystallized figs. Of course, it may all be coincidence. We asked the porter, but he speaks no German. I am resting behind the fourth window from the left on the third floor of the small chateau in the foreground. Remember there are only four more days.

Tristan da Cunha *Sybil to Runciman*

The midget submarines are already off Corsica. The Bishop will send you full instructions by the helicopter. If Bridget won't believe you, wire for a new propeller. And keep the lines clear. The ball is at everyone's feet now.

Neueschwanstein

Sir Roger Green
to Rodrigo

I arrived yesterday. The soap is atrocious. From my bedroom window I can see the bridge which Wagner mentions in Parsifal. How Eric kept the Exchequer intact is a mystery. Remember that if all else fails we may still be able to enter Liechtenstein by the cable-car.

Fort Worth

The Bishop
to Amos Long

I have had to work my electric razor from the light socket. The *son et lumière* is magnificent but the rockets have kept me awake half the night. Watch out for the movements of the Baltic Squadron. I anticipate a disastrous fall in consols. My blessing to Peter and Paul.

Mexico City

Miss Emily
Nonesince to
Commander Singal

The new stamps are extremely indecent. They show the *voladores* with nothing on but wings. I know the camera works, but we cannot afford to take any risks. I shall try to get a message through by the Thunderbird. We must be patient, *Liebchen*.

Montevideo

Ludovic
Meyer Smith to
Miss Emily Nonesince

I apologize for the cigarette burn. This morning our embassy was incinerated by the Czech insurgents. Mountjoy has taken refuge in the docks. We shall try to ship him out in an orange-box. I recommend a red alert for the passenger pigeons.

Ballyshannon   *The Bishop*
to Earl Boyes

The Portuguese destroyers have relieved Marangatam. Sir Giles was caught – quite literally – with his trousers down. The Exchange is cock-a-hoop. I have put my shirt on gilt-edged. What a lovely thing the Bloody Foreland is!

Melbourne   *Perrutz and*
Nellie to Sir Roger Green

Mandryk is inconsolable. An anarchist has poisoned one of these bears with a eucalyptus leaf. How is Natchka? The Sydney papers are full of the gliding trials on Helvellyn. I think the imperial fleet will move in the Baltic.

Ottawa   *Sir Lucas Crowther*
to Otto van Fleet

Do you know that when the French advanced they picked out Jeremy by his green cockade? I believe the Orangemen are still at bay in the Maddermarket. Why ever did Nancy paint them in slick greys? Fenris has learnt to bark in Morse. But the sky is black with Finnish caravelles.

Salt Lake City   *Rodrigo*
to Courtelle

This morning Boris was killed by an air-gun pellet outside the Tabernacle. The police have made extensive inquiries but no-one can shed any light on either the motive or the possible culprit. As you see, it is a long building a little like a sugar loaf. I have suffered a mild recurrence of orchitis. Perhaps I shall buy a chihuahua.

Amalfi *Sprock to the Captain*
In the Cloister of Paradise this morning I encountered a small boy with a wen. He is not, of course, in the picture. Gretchen has bought a bikini embroidered with turtles in white silk. For breakfast yesterday we ate a new species of cray-fish. Alaric is well.

Mykonos *Lord Maundy to Miss Anstruther*
We are surely safe here, not three miles from Apollo's lions. I have hired myself a flat in the village. It is all yellow now, from the rays. If the Captain rings tonight, I am ready. Believe me, Gwendoline, we are going under with all flags flying.

Pitcairn Island *Commander Singal to Squadron Leader Baring*
We boarded the ss *Paradise* off Tongareva. The crew put up a stiff fight, but we cracked the hold. There were forty-three Malayan rifles in banana cases. Now do you see we must intervene in Penang? I am writing this full steam ahead for Guayaquil.

Entebbe *Solly Jaggers to the Queen of Windhoek*
The Albertville Regatta was a great success. Our probation officers were the pride of Mozambique in their coonskin loincloths. This turbulence in the zinc mines must soon subside. Majesty, we are both in up to our necks. But wait and see, we shall laugh together in Broken Hill.

Basalt Springs *Adolphus Pratt to Squadron Leader Baring*
We are eight thousand feet above Copenhagen. Observe the clarity of the air. I have ridden all morning in a Western saddle. At night our satellites are like gems in the Queen of Sheba's diadem. I know we shall win.

Rotterdam *Miss Anstruther to Courtelle*
The marijuana was in the joystick. You had better make your getaway in the Puss Moth. I suggest a straight course over Chesham and Princes Risborough. Remember what Jacob said. There is no meaning or purpose; only the codes.

Lyme Regis *Morgan Everest to Sir Linstock Esher*
They will get me in five minutes. I have four slugs left. Here in the Shell Tower, my leader, the last outpost of Western values is crumbling. What wouldn't I give for a thimbleful of tequila! Christ, they are coming.

Havana *Sir Linstock Esher to Alvarez da Sala*
War has broken out with Albania. The Guatemalan auxiliaries have embarked in the Q-boat. I see no hope of a victory at Rifa Chiffa. Here on the quay the Chinese laundrymen are in arms for new mangles. A reward is out for Angus McFlyte.

King George V Land *Felix Emberton to Miss Alison Peery*

I have bound your *Meditations* in sealskin. The hovercraft is an asset, but what shall we do for bear-spears? The prefabricated igloos were not a success. The last John Collinson is alive with woodmites. Dear Alison, I am snow-blind, I cannot see the Winkles.

Astrakhan *The Bishop to Lynx Raffles*

Canadian Javelins have dropped four points. I am transferring a million rupees to Hercules Powder. The MSS are safe in Foochow. Who knows which way the mandarins will jump? I played a hand of mah-jong with Clovis yesterday.

Wanganui *Clovis to Alaric*

The boys have taken the whole thing very well. We all went into the shelters singing the *Te Deum*. Runciman smashed the RG2 but we got the second stanza on the ribbon mike. I am very puzzled about the news from the Swiss border. How ever does Atalanta hope to win?

Groningen *Earl Boyes to Sister Eakins*

It is sealing wax, not blood, my darling. I have had to melt it over a paraffin lamp in the larder. Whiskers shall have a tin of ginger biscuits, but not for another day. Tonight I can think of nothing except our defeat in the Estuary of the Plate. They say the Amazons were superb.

Porsanger Fjord *Alvarez da Sala to Ensign Lascelles*

Our ambassador has handed an ultimatum to the Gambian Foreign Minister. There is no hope of a settlement with the Greeks. If the English back their minelayers in the Skagerrak, we are done for. I am playing gin rummy with a Lapp chiropodist. Grizelda has had poor hands.

Vaduz *Courtelle to Rivers*

Our armed forces have multiplied eight times. Here they are in their goatskin tunics. Given but resolution, we could hold the pass for thirteen days with pea-shooters. What news, by the way, of Lynx Raffles? The Prince relies on his total annihilation of the Kurds at Orenburg.

Curaçao *The Queen of Windhoek to the Captain*

The artificial whale is already inside the harbour. Momssen has cabled that every man will do his duty. Five, four, three, two, one, zero. That was it. Congratulate me, Solly, the whole of Bolivia is in Javan hands.

Starbuck Island *The Queen of Windhoek to The Captain*

The PGN commando has landed at West Point. Sir Hilary has held the four beaches, but Nathan says it is only time. I remember once at Cape Farewell we beat them back with soup-ladles. Here by the swamp I can smell the peccaries. I am not enamoured of a life of whale steaks.

101

Pretoria   *Lynx Raffles to*
Morgan Everest

The Glue Factory is already under pressure. These damned Watutsi take some grinding-down. The over-print is a joke, of course, but they do need volunteers. I am dead beat. They taught me the word for jig-a-jig in Swahili.

Sevastopol   *The Captain*
to Favorita

I believe Mountjoy was shot with a German-ground Beretta. The ace of spades was found tucked in his left trouser turn-up. I have had to live on caviare. And this view of the Black Sea is not original. Still, we persist.

Grootfontein   *Elvira*
Norman to
Simon Hardcastle

I have caught and tamed a whistling hyena. Alas, his dung is the colour of grapefruit juice. First it was fluoride and now these pills. I would willingly drown the Queen of Windhoek in her African cointreau. Have these people no shame?

San Marino   *Canon*
Slocombe to
Amos Long

The zeppelins were a fine sight from the rampart. How I wonder what Raymond Allister would have thought! We played a few hands of bézique once in the *pensione*. He was always a lover of good cigars. Remember to send my driving licence.

Dar es Salaam   *Tregenza*
to Sigmund

You remember what Nietschze said about the tortoise? This is it. I have never eaten so many betel-nuts in my life. The jeeps are still hunting for Peregrine in the Bong. The rhinoceros detail has withdrawn, of course, but the compensation is still a very open question.

Easter Island   *Sangster*
and Forbes to
Canon Slocombe

We saw the bombers go overhead this morning. It seemed as if all the gods were craning their necks to look. I have finished the second volume of your Treitschke. There is no more moving analysis in the language. We are spending most of our time in the sea.

Amritsar   *Strangeways*
to Manley

There are strikes in the manganese refinery. The polo ponies are dying of rickets at Simla. They tell me that Crazy Horse has escaped from Berlinnie. With that hair-do he can hardly hire a jaguar. Still, it is no smiling matter.

Novosibirsk   *Runciman to*
Ludovic Meyer Smith

We are out of shillings for the gas-meter. I am writing this in my bala-clava. Even the opera has closed. I shall try to break the road-blocks with a snow plough. But I think we are trapped.

Angmagsalik   *Nicholas*
Emery to Professor Stolz

The last Arabian was four feet tall. We found his body three hundred yards from the filling station. There were skeletons of a hundred mice in the spars of a bran tub. They must have had it rough. Remember me to Mrs Noakes.

Beersheba   *Julius Andover*
to Simon Hardcastle

I deeply regret the news from Helsingfors. If the barricades are up in the flea-market, let Felix Emberton retire. I know my longhand is appalling, but persevere, Simon. I am bleeding from the groin. And they shot my secretary.

Peking   *Ensign Lascelles*
to the
Burgomaster of Coventry

I have burned a hole in my sou'wester with the electric iron. The perils of travelling! I have just heard the news. The giant pandas have stripped the bamboo forests as far as Kanchenjunga. What on earth can have caused this population explosion?

Mauritius   *Sir Lucas*
Crowther to
the Captain

I am sheltering in the smallest room of the Lithuanian consulate. Forgive my handwriting. The illuminations are distracting. Jellaby did all he could, but the zebra-men were too much. In five minutes I shall make a dash for the mail van.

Taormina   *Amos Long to*
Patch Codron

I can hear the Greek maids hoovering the Captain's bedroom. I hope the bloodstrains will respond to the spot lifter. It was quite a party. We got the first four with the Maxim gun, but Repetto escaped in the bread-lift. To think that Garibaldi set out from such a tiny bay!

South Shields   *McFlayle*
to Mr Evans

I am on my way to the Richmond Trailer Festival. There are broken Rileys in all the lay-bys. For an hour and a half we shall pay our homage to Wisley and Deans. If only Algy would use the apple and biscuit mine. We could break the Tay Boom with a single charge.

Paranagua   *Favorita to*
Lord Maundy

I have won four thousand milreis at the animal game. Alicia had bought a handbag of ostrich-skin, so I played the crocodile. One should never jump to conclusions. They say da Sala has broken all records at the Durban Book Fair. My respects to the Duke of Tandy.

Kanazawa   *Mrs Noakes*
to the
Duke of Tandy

Away we go on my new Corona Marauder! And what a victory for our men in the Hinge of Borneo! The Creole paratroops are already shelling the Community Centre. Here on the sixth floor I can hear the volcano. I must try sleeping with ear-plugs.

Aberdeen *Repetto to Sprock*

The herring-boats are full of poisoned mackerel. The dead lobster is in the creel. I am typing this to be shown at once to Elvira Norman. Tell your beads, my dear, for a sick retriever. And keep your fingers crossed.

Castelvetrano *Millicent to Sir Lucas Crowther*

I am reading the sonnets of Gertrude Thimbleby. There is nothing like them in English. Father, I know, you are off to Mangalore. Let Amber advance one single reason why this koati should die. I am ill with hate.

Conway Castle *Lieutenant Flyte to Commander Singal*

We are down to the last barrel of apples. Bartholomew has fled. The men are living on dead mice. I have tested the life-belts, but even the rubber has perished. I am emptied of everything except the desire to hold out for another day.

Palermo *Sigmund to Perrutz and Nellie*

This morning my hearing aid was broken at Monreale. I can hardly believe it was an accident. In the Corpus Christi procession Vencini spat in the gutter as he passed below their posters. Here at the Britannique the sea-food is excellent. But how can it last?

The Return

    After the light has set
First I imagine silence: then the stroke
As if some drum beat outside has come in.
And in the silence I smell moving smoke
And feel the touch of coarse cloth on my skin.
    And all is darkness yet
Save where the hot wax withers by my chin.

    When I had fallen (bone
Bloodying wet stone) he would lead me back
Along the street and up the corkscrew stair

104

(Time running anti-clockwise, fingers slack)
And open windows to let in fresh air
    And leave me stretched alone
With sunken cheeks drained whiter than my hair.

    Then I was young. Before
Another stroke he will come back in bone
And thin my heart. That soot-black hill will break
And raise him in his clay suit from the stone
While my chalk-ridden fingers dryly ache
    And burn. On this rush floor
He will come striding hotly. When I wake

    The stroke will have been tolled
And I shall take his crushed purse in my hand
And feel it pulse (warm, empty) on my wrist.
Blood floods my temples. Clay man, from what land
Have you come back to keep your freezing tryst
    With someone grown so old?
Soldier, forgive me. Candles die in mist.

    And now a cold wind stirs
Inside the shuttered room. I feel his hand
Brushing the stale air, feeling for my place
Across the phlegm-soaked pillows. I am sand
Threading a glass with slow and even pace
    And dying in my furs.
My father turns, with tears on his young face.

A Dirge

I killed you where the coastal road
Fled from the hills. And, cradled in my hands,
 Your bony face, clenched still in pride,
 Bled in the waves. All that was owed
Is wiped in this blind striking on the sands,
  I thought; but through your side

I felt the sea of death creep in
From all your broken caves of slate and stone
 And lick the shore. Eight million stood
 In mourning for your scar of skin
And hair, shell-bred frigidity of bone,
  Each bare of his black hood.

And club-foot children stooped to kiss
Those rubbered hands that pressed them through the steel
 With tears on their grey cheeks. Old men,
 Remembering the cold fire's hiss
Through burning olives, paused to bow and kneel
  Beside your body. Then

I alone rose, unpitying, cold.
Sure that some kinsman stared me in your face
 I limped through ashen files of blood
 And parted from the dust of old
Men ebbing from my own swell-footed pace.
  Blind to the mounting flood

Of corpses, I limped through and on
Beyond the last revived wave to that land
 You once ruled. There a black dog rolled
 By a cold hearth whose fire had gone.

And I remembered how it licked my hand
    When I was in your fold.

The Land-Mine

It fell when I was sleeping. In my dream
    It brought the garden to the house
And let it in. I heard no parrot scream
    Or lion roar, but there were flowers
And water flowing where the cellared mouse
Was all before. And air moved as in bowers

Of cedar with a scented breath of smoke
    And fire. I rubbed scales from my eyes
And white with brushed stone in my hair half-woke
    In fear. I saw my father kneel
On glass that scarred the ground. And there were flies
Thick on that water, weeds around his heel

Where he was praying. And I knew that night
    Had cataracted through the wall
And loosed fine doors whose hinges had been tight
    And made each window weep glass tears
That clawed my hands. I climbed through holes. My hall
Where I had lain asleep with stoppered ears

Was all in ruins, planted thick with grime
    Of war. I walked as if in greaves
Through fire, lay down in gutters choked with lime
    And spoke for help. Alas, those birds

That dived in light above me in the leaves
Were birds of prey, and paid no heed to words.

Now I was walking, wearing on my brow
    What moved before through fireless coal
And held my father's head. I touch it now
    And feel my dream go. And no sound
That flying birds can make, or burrowing mole,
Will bring my garden back, or break new ground.

The war is over and the mine has gone
    That filled the air with whinnying fire
And no more nights will I lie waiting on
    Cold metal or cold stone to freeze
Before it comes again. That day of ire,
If it shall come, will find me on my knees.

The Shell

Since the shell came and took you in its arms
    Whose body was fine bone
That walked in light beside a place of flowers,
    Why should your son
Years after the eclipse of those alarms
    Perplex this bitten stone
For some spent issue of the sea? Not one
Blue drop of drying blood I could call ours

In all that ocean that you were remains
    To move again. I come

Through darkness from a distance to your tomb
    And feel the swell
Where a dark flood goes headlong to the drains.
    I hear black hailstones drum
Like cold slugs on your skin. There is no bell
To tell what drowned king founders. Violets bloom

Where someone died. I dream that overhead
    I hear a bomber drone
And feel again stiff pumping of slow guns
    Then the all-clear's
Voice break, and the long summing of the dead
    Below the siren's moan
Subdue the salt flood of all blood and tears
To a prolonged strained weeping sound that stuns.

I turn in anger. By whatever stars
    Clear out of drifting rack
This winter evening I revive my claim
    To what has gone
Beyond your dying fall. Through these cold bars
    I feel your breaking back
And live again your body falling on
That flood of stone where no white Saviour came

On Christian feet to lift you to the verge
    Or swans with wings of fire
Whose necks were arched in mourning. Black as coal
    I turn to go
Out of the graveyard. Headstone shadows merge
    And blur. I see the spire
Lift over corpses. And I sense the flow
Of death like honey to make all things whole.

The Ward

Along that ward men died each winter night.
    One in an iron lung
Used to cry out before that salving tin
Strapped round his breathing stifled him. One hung
        In a strange brace
That moved his dead leg gently. And no light
    Out of that blaze where Hitler in
His burning concrete died lit the cramped face

Of a boy paralysed. I in that war
    Lay with cold steel on wrists
Recording how my heart beat, saved and one
With the men dying. Dark amidst the mists
        Across the seas
Each night in France those armies gripped and tore
    Each other's guts out, and no sun
Arched in at dawn through stiff windows to ease

Men left in pain. Sisters on morning rounds
    Brought laundered sheets and screens
Where they were needed. And when doctors came
In clean coats with their talk and their machines,
        Behind their eyes
Moving to help, what was there? To the sounds
    Of distant gunfire, in our name,
So many men walked into death. What lies

And festers is the wastage. Here the beast
    Still breathes its burning stone
And claws the entrails. And those hours of cold
When I lay waking, hearing men alone
        Fight into death

Swim back and grip. And I feel rise like yeast
    A sense of the whole world grown old
With no-one winning. And I fight for breath.

An Elegy

Last night I dreamed you came back. In my cot
Of cane I kicked, squat fingers curled like ferns
    Around your beads. I was just one
And needed things to clutch. Too late one learns
    (Love passing) all we miss in what
We reach to hold. This morning, in the sun

Along that crowded street, I walked and saw
The ether clear, and your keen face etched through
    As if on glass. Under the glaze
Of pre-war Kodak in my blood-book, you
    (As in my mind's eye) pose and thaw
Before my father's hands. In furs you laze

Beside his 30s car with filled-in wheels
While picnic-baskets open. You drink tea
    On grass. Then by a rock you stand
Staring at sepia water. And with me
    In tow, throw bread to leaping seals
(That must be Glasgow) smiling. Sun and sand

Open their honeyed vistas, and the war
Swims under water, years away. I turn
    Pages of pity. Here I sit

With Mac who licked my face when I was born
And died for worrying sheep. A door
Into my father's death parts. Here you knit

A fair-isle jersey for him, here link arms
With arms in khaki, here take off his hat
And kiss his thin hair. Were you pleased
In this one where you seem to laugh and chat
As he drives off? And what alarms
You in this weirdly blurred one? Were you seized

By fear or simply dazzled? There's no end
To all they hint. Each thick page in my brain
Erupts and bleeds. Rich blood of kin,
Dense with the war, wells upwards like a stain
Through all my strange thoughts. And no bend
In sleep or waking movement folds it in

Or stops him dying. Blood is in my veins
From things that happened in your body where
His cool hands touched it, where I lay
Before my birth. In you I climbed a stair
Whose treads were water, wearing chains
Of ropes of flesh that I was free to fray,

Though not to break. And when my birth day came
I could swing out. And there in light I broke
And stood bare-naked. I was king
Of all the flowers and sunlight by one stroke
Of silver blades. I owned his name
And both your blood. Tonight on blood I bring

My anchored body from his broken back
To your thrown side. I count the standing men
And watch their whispers. Through the door

I hear you weeping. Someone sees me. Then
    They take me in. I sense the crack
In our closed wall and cry for you. Then your

Own time is here. I come to your pale side
And enter in. So many miles of stone
    After that sea I have to walk
Before I reach you! Why is your clean bone
    So bare? Has the receding tide
Sucked all your living tissue, left me chalk

Where nothing grows? No brilliant cells I see,
No poison dew. Death's music plays in green
    On inner ground so often. Growth
Lush as below the sea. Not here. No sheen
    Of dense bloom gathers. That would be
Some bright relief from this blue stone. On both

Sides of your body I confront chalk, find
Only the barren, scentless, tasteless rock
    Of your dry death. So I return
(Dreams passing into day) through glass. I lock
    Your stone wood in my inward mind
And come alive. I feel hot coffee burn,

Laving my throat. I lie on green brocade
Stretched over cane, reflecting. Fifteen hours
    It is since I was in that sleep
Where you were living still. Do any flowers
    Bloom on your grave? I hear a spade
Grate over clay. Years later, I can weep

Only for your belongings: a green jar,
A crocodile-skin hand-bag, a long brush
    That touched your hair. I hold it here

113

And scrape some living tissue. I could rush
   To tears. I think bereaved men are
Too far at sea in grief for this. How clear

In blood of mind can I be, losing love
At such a distance? Here above your hair
   I know the way to learn. I lie
Broad waking on my cool bed. I am bare
   As he was with you. High above
On this first night I feel wind stroke the sky

And stir my skin. Close by I hear the tune
Of falling rain. And when your body comes
   In gauze like sea-mist from the shore
At morning, I put out my sails from slums
   To clean sea. And below the moon
I enter you in joy, as none before.

The Blade

I see her walking on the lawn in white,
   Her feet bare in the ground.
Above her in her room her joss-sticks burn
Rich in an air that lives with dying sound.
I watch hot smoke surround her in the light
     As in an urn.

Then she is writing, and I watch her write,
   Her hand bare on the sheet.
Against her window she has found a bat

114

That beats its wings to breaking in the heat
To be let in. I watch her toes grow tight
   On the straw mat.

Then she is walking, and I see her pause,
  Her face bare in the glass.
Above her arm I see the raven blue,
Its gouged holes ready for the thing to pass
And let her go. I watch her touch the doors
   No light comes through.

Then I am reading, and I smell the blood,
  Her words bare in my hand.
Then she is talking, and I read her talk
In open purple on a folded band
Where ink has whipped and curdled into mud
   I start to walk.

Then I am with her in the razored air,
  Her tongue bare in my lips.
Under her black thin silks I touch the blade,
Hearing the cracked sink spit where water drips.
Then, where the first light comes, I kiss her hair
   And wake afraid.

The Avocado Plant

Where you were planted, clouds hung low and grey
Over the clinic roof. She was too sick
  To dig your stone deep. No thin ray

115

Of quick sun pierced her locked room. Moist and thick
In claustrophobic darkness you grew strong
        And stretched. Those long

Drooping and furrowed leaves, clasped round your stem
And leaned against her peeling walls now, swept
    Up in confined space. Choked with phlegm,
She coughed in cloying heat you throve on, wept
In dry air. Now she grows through barren light
        Where you hang, tight

In all your cells, green leaves turned ashen-grey
And spoiled by wax. Where candles tint her air
    She lies, white-naked. Far away,
Glass-clear in distance, she can hear the flare
Of open gas-jets. Turning to the wall
        I feel her fall

Into my present, and my skin. Her hand
That moves in even silence, twitches, grips
    And stirs the dark scent. She is fanned
Across far water by the wind on lips
She parts on cloth. You die beside her, dark
        As she was dark

In those deep months of nothing. Now the light
In this dense flat, half-open to the sun,
    Rasps your cold skin. You cry for night
For your rough fruits. Your children, one by one,
Falter, are picked. I touch one with my tongue
        In secret, stung

By such bared harshness. Acid in the mouth
You are, dark plant. And in the groin too hard
    For her. I feel her breathe. Far south

Of here you flowered once. As soft as lard
Your dark flesh felt then. Raped of your last stone
    You die alone

Now in the light. Across her flustered bed
She reaches with her finger to your soil
   And stirs your roots. She who has shed
All of her fever in the flex of oil
Lets her hair fall across your leaves. Her breath
        Quickens your death.

The Heir

   I took him in. One winter night
The wheels we hired were stayed on wet stone. Light
Flared in the stucco. Silent on the stair,
   Linked arm in arm, we rose
As warm air in our crowded house to where
The high room in the darkness held and froze

   White head to head. There, cool in sheets
That smelt of man-sweat, stripped of all my heats,
I lay in rustling, tasting mint and wine
   From his long tongue, and with his hand
Soft on my rough skin, felt his naked spine
And then his groin move, and my shoulder fanned

   By dry hair brushing me. Then rain
Broke on the windows, broke, and broke again
In hissing spikes at war with wrinkling tin

My flesh was heir to. Trembling, tense,
I lay in my thin sheath, locked in a skin
Too scarce to keep the storm out. Every sense

Whimpered for pity. I could hear
The bat-squeal, smell the owl-spit, taste the clear
Blood of the mice that split between the claws
I touched. But what I saw was bone
White on the ground where corpses, fouled with straws,
Worked on each other. So I took one stone

Out of the hail that washed and filed
My attic window, and I made this child
To lie in flesh so rich with pleasure, blades
Of grass could take it. Here it lies,
Hard, wrinkled as a dried fruit's. And what shades
It with his body, is the wind that dies.

Prayer to the White Lady

*after Himnusz Minden Idoben
by Laszlo Nagy*

I

Creature of flame, out of
the sun's bow I call you:
moment of crystal for the throwing-knife,
    *lighten my darkness, I
need you now.*

118

II

O, lady of the small larks,
keeper of the instruments
in the zenith, last room of the king,
  lighten my darkness, I
need you now.

III

Palm in the rain of sorrow,
fire under glaze, lifting
the twin domes of your body above me,
  lighten my darkness, I
need you now.

IV

Mistress of Victory, flame
of the gathering storm, brightening
into the jails of my eyes,
  lighten my darkness, I
need you now.

V

Nurse of the war-wounded, yours is
the house of the Jew and the Negro:
draught of the bee's kiss, mysterious honey,
  lighten my darkness, I
need you now.

VI

Lady, oblivious of blood and money,
belly-dancer of hunger, echo
and resonance of the millennium,

lighten my darkness, I
need you now.

VII

O, my dear one, tempered
by the beam of the laser, torn
by the stone body of the gorgon, the man-child,
  lighten my darkness, I
need you now.

VIII

Always your tall house was open to me,
glittering with expectation: O, godlike
above the bronze cauldron of your beauty,
  lighten my darkness, I
need you now.

IX

In the beginning I felt your body lap me,
drowning into the saraband of love:
killer of the black crows that haunt me,
  lighten my darkness, I
need you now.

X

Now, on the brink of the vacuum, at the edge
where the million tendrils of nothingness
are erupting, even out of my own mind,
  lighten my darkness, I
need you now.

XI

Lady of pain, sharer of this affliction,
sufferer under the same electric coil:
now, as I reach for the dark pill and the needle,
  lighten my darkness, I
need you now.

XII

Only in you will the house of my body glisten
gold in all its chimneys and veins:
only in you will the white pigeons flicker,
  lighten my darkness, I
need you now.

To Eurydice in Hell

I

Then Orpheus walked in a dark
forest of books and people
thinking of nothing, but

when Eurydice came the leaves
paused on the trees
to listen, the wet snail

cocked its horn, it was
morning everywhere
in the pulsing wood

he called pleasure and
the sun shone. To be stones
rolling in dark brooks

was a new beginning and
dead things broke into flower.
So Orpheus sang.

II

But Eurydice walked in
a close alliance with
nothing, that watched

her. Only the song
of Orpheus could make
her real, and that not

for long. For nine days
the bad core of Eurydice
rotted, but on the tenth

Eurydice died,
and the whole inside of
her moved into hell

where she lay as naked as
nothing. Only
the flesh of Eurydice stayed

alive. And the nothing within her
came out and gashed its name
in her belly, that

122

bled for Orpheus. Take
away the bones, there is
nothing to hold

Eurydice. Take away
the skin, she has no passport
for the lonely wood

where Orpheus sings. Praise
her in razor-blades, it is
only through pain that

brings pleasure that
sad Eurydice lives now.
So Orpheus sang.

III

Then Orpheus came into hell, who
had no love for the mad
and hated the blind silence

there. And the darkness
reached out its arms
and wrapped Orpheus too

in its chloroform. And he spoke
with dread mud and
water to let

her go. Prayed to
the hot bands in the wall
that they might

leave her. Hands are a spoiled
nuisance, they
pull the soul out. Stay

123

away, Orpheus, here there is only
the rule of nothing. Eurydice
has gone into skin, she is

no one here. Look.
There is no one here.
So Orpheus sang.

IV

Alas, there is only
tomorrow the black
nowhere to go in

now, is that
it? Walk, Orpheus, by
the sounding Thames. Your head

the black nurse struck
from your future sticks
like a heart

in the hospital, you
have no brain now
for the world you live

in, it bleeds
in the cold river
Eurydice has dissolved into

you call hell. But look, Orpheus,
Eurydice is a star
whose face kisses your

bloody lips in the
water. You two are
at one now, in the sky.

So Orpheus sang,
believing nothing,
to Eurydice in hell.

The World of the Oboe

I

To be entering, then, the
   whorled avalanche
of raw porcelain we call
   the ear. I am privileged,

I go in, I step with care.
   Bats flap in the
stone heights, there are lizards
   moist over bare toes. In

a green corner luxuriant
   succulents weep. Here heat
shakes hands with cold in
   a taunting alliance. Where lips

open, tastes knot
   and unreel in
a tract of eddying
   flavours, blazing

125

like seaweed. Over a carpet
    of scuffling insects, in
torrid anticipation (such intermediaries!)
    I go into it.

II

I am cool (but not cold) following
    the scent through brakes
where it fell in patches: frost
    on the grass, twigs, lips: flat out
over hard earth: creeping
    between low branches, a
twist – spiral of acrid smoke
    in the chimney of wet
noses: draught of
    invisible lime
in long throats: the Delft flick
    of a grey brush
tinting in watercolours.

III

    With so many holes
in the wood
    to choose from, which
will it hide in?
    Slipping
bright-eyed, and
    alert to the
touch of others, heels,
    hooves and a
pad pad pad of the hounds now
    dwindling

whiskers, prick-ears, the body of it and
   tail tip
into nothing.

       IV

         (If
  Mies, paring the
slivers of white lava
  to fine liths, is
more, this
  is less.)

       v

The needle is running
  now in and out in and
out over the canvas: a prickle of
  (is it fear? is it expectation?) as
archers come tumbling. Under the Latin

Harold is red silk, and the arrow
  enters his eye: and the iron eye
leaps and is looping
  under and over. Between and below
the blunt fingers

gather and follow the pattern
  Odo sets them. It threads
yellow green blue and the cloth
  stiffens with Norman horses. Their hooves
go clop a clop clop a clop

all interlacing. Two
  cultures are dancing in blithe

liaison. Already the needle
   dips, leaps and is bright,
silver-scaled, in the sunlight.

VI

Burning in darkness it
   cuts to a vague
blur of oranges: waxed
   apple with a black
wick, the globed
   candle fits in its
iron tripod (splayed
   rubber legs
erect it) and how

the blue essence
   whirled in a wind
from the kitchen stirs,
   flicks and is hot
on the close fingers, no
   wit can
interpret. It laves
   the cold air
with a salve of

imperial calm. So
   muted, licked,
swivelling between
   the wide area it
commands the allegiance
   of warmth from, it
swings like incense
   in a dark aisle
where fruit kneels.

VII

Outside the snow falls in a mindless blank
where the downward turn
is all the hand can feel. If she lifts

her face (the girl in the glass cage) she is old
enough to be tasting
the dipped salt on her tongue. The forgotten sea

drips into the grained skin that is ready
for it. So many crystals
of grey light in the sugar sifter of

steel sponges! The nose hurts, it is
pressurized by the freezing point
of anonymous water. Come in, Mercy, no

other name in the bleak roll of
the Norse winter
interrogates the moment your head rests in.

VIII

A filled thing. It is heavy
with what some
acceptable remonstrance
would call

honey, if that were a sap
yielded like bone
from the ice
fur is gathered in:

odour of musk (or
is it goat-butter the

129

dogs, ravening,
were driven wild by?)

IX

So over and over the spider turns
   in the air of
the dry hall. It is waiting
   for something to break,
spin, collapse in its web
   of connections. The glazed heads
bend in the pit, there
   are things fluttering
above the holes in the wood. It
   will happen soon. So
many imprisoned below that
   alert vegetable, they
have to get out. The spider
   has filled the room, there
is no gap for it all
   to start again. That dangerous order
has taken over the sphere
   it always can, and the
world of the oboe (flies,
   why else do we call
them flies in a
   walnut shell, they are always
escaping) been snapped
   suddenly, effortlessly, shut.

Bats

have no accidents. They loop
their incredible horse-shoe
loops, dead-stop

on air-brakes,
road-safe on
squeaks: racketeering

their SOS noise in a
jai-alai
bat-jam

of collapsed umbrellas, a
Chancery Lane
of avoided

collisions, all in a
cave without lights: then
hung

happy, a snore
of strap-hangers
undergrounding

without an *Evening
Standard* between them
to the common Waterloo

that awaits bats, like
all beasts, then
off now, zoom!

Man, you can't even
hear them; bats,
are they?

What Metre Is

it is a matter
of counting (five
syllables in the first line, four
in the second) and

so on. Or we can change to
seven words in the first line
six in the second. Is
that arbitrary?

Prose is another possibility. There could be three
sentences in the stanza. This would be an example of
that.

Which (on the other hand)
we could lay out
by a letter count, as (this by the way is
free verse, without metre)

'pro
se is another possib
ility. There could be th
ree sent
ences in the st

anza. This would be an exam
ple of that.' I mean
it is a matter
of mathematics. Intervals between
the words, three to
a line is the
rule here. It results

in the same as
having words, four to
a line. In the
mind of the poet,
though, it makes a
difference. White spaces
(now it is two spaces) are

just articulation,
space, words
(now it
is one)

mean
something

(now
it
is
words) and

no it is
not
music either. Internal
rhyming (though sometimes
the kernel of new ideas) is
a matter of timing.

The same is true for
rhythm, the beat
(two to a line
it is here)

only becomes like a rhythm when
as here it moves with a regular
dactyl or two to a line. If

slow now spondees
make lines move, stiff
rhythm is metre (in dactyls again) but
rhythm is usually not
like this. In a word

it can escalate
drop

do as it pleases
move freely
(look out, I'm coming)

stop
at a stop

and so on. Assonance
that semblance
(except in Owen)
a, when

it works, echo
of awkwardness is O.K.

but not for me: nor is lively
alliteration

leaping
long lean and allusive
through low lines. It

becomes a matter
of going back
to metre, ending w

ith its mos
t irrit
ating (perhaps) manif
estation thi
s inarticul
ate mechanical stu
tter. It is the voi
ce of the type-wr
iter. It is the abdic
ation of insp

iration. I li
ke it. It i
s the logica

i exp
ression o
f itsel
f.

At the House of Jade

from the Chinese of Fan Chung Yen (AD *989–1052*)

'leaves drifting – cold – house empty – absence – lamp-light –
loneliness'

SL   IF
EE   T.
V

E
S   I
DR   HO

        US
        E
        A

        B
        SE
        NC

        E.

        L

        I
        GH
        T

        IN
         L
        O

N
EL
Y

CO
LD

,

LA
MP

L
EA
V

E
S
ME

L
ES
S

OL
D

LE
AV
E

S
.
E

AV
ES

E
MP
TY

A
MP
L
E
L
IE
S.

H

O
W
I

KN
OW
!

E
VE

'S
R
I

F
T
AL

ON
E
L

I
ES
  D

RI
FT
I

N
G,
  L

IG
HT

I
N
EM

PT
Y
C

O
LD
.

I
S
H

I
FT
 H

OU
SE
,

LI
GH

T
MY

L
AM
P.

IF

S
HE
 I

S
AB
S

E
NC
E,

   L
EA
V

E
S
DR

IF
T
I

N   (2–2–1
  M   1–2–2
E.   alternately)

Pavan for an Unborn Infanta

AN-AN CHI-CHI
AN-AN CHI-CHI

CHI-CHI AN-AN
CHI-CHI AN-AN

CHI-AN

CHI-AN CHI-AN CHI-AN CHI-AN CHI
AN-CHI AN-CHI AN-CHI AN

CHI-AN CHI-AN CHI-AN CHI-AN CHI
AN-CHI AN-CHI AN-CHI AN

CHI-AN

AN-CHI AN-CHI AN-CHI AN
AN-CHI AN-CHI AN-CHI AN

CHI-CHI

AN-AN CHI-CHI
AN-AN CHI-CHI

CHI-CHI AN-AN
CHI-CHI AN-AN

AN-AN

AN-AN AN-AN AN-AN AN-AN

CHI-CHI CHI-CHI CHI-CHI
CHI-CHI CHI-CHI CHI-CHI

CHI-CHI

AN-AN AN-AN
AN-AN AN-AN

AN-AN AN-AN
AN-AN AN-AN

AN-AN

CHI-CHI CHI-CHI
CHI-CHI CHI-CHI

CHI-CHI CHI-CHI
CHI-CHI CHI-CHI

CHI-CHI

The Lax Cheer

                        I

                        ro
                        be
                        rt
                            l
                        ax

                            r
                        ob
                        er
                        t
                        la
                        x

                        ro
                        be
                        rt

143

l
ax

r
ob
er
t
la
x

ro
be
rt
l
ax

r
ob
er
t
la
x

II
la
x

la
x

la
x

III

r
ob
er
t

r
ob
er
t

IV

l
ax

l
ax

v

ro
be
rt

ro
be
rt

vi

l
ax
r
ob

er
t

la
x
ro
be
rt

l
ax
r
ob
er
t

la
x
ro
be
rt

l
ax
r
ob
er
t

la

x
ro
be
rt

Fourteen Ways
of Touching the Peter

I

You can push
your thumb
in the
ridge
between his
shoulder-blades
to please him.

II

Starting
at its root,
you can let
his whole
tail
flow
through your hand.

III

Forming
a fist
you can let
him rub
his bone
skull
against it, hard.

IV

When he makes
bread,
you can lift
him
by his under-
sides on your
knuckles.

V

In hot
weather
you can itch
the fur
under
his chin. He
likes that.

VI

At night
you can hoist
him
out of his bean-stalk,
sleepily

clutching
paper bags.

VII

Pressing
his head against
your cheek,
you can carry
him
in the dark,
safely.

VIII

In late autumn
you can find
seeds
adhering
to his fur.
There are
plenty.

IX

You can prise
his jaws
open,
helping
any medicine
he won't
abide, go down.

X

You can touch
his
feet, only

if
he is relaxed.
He
doesn't like it.

XI

You can comb
spare thin
fur
from his coat,
so he won't
get
fur-ball.

XII

You can shake
his rigid
chicken-leg leg,
scouring his
hind-quarters
with his Vim
tongue.

XIII

Dumping
hot fish
on his plate, you can
fend
him off,
pushing
and purring.

You can have
him shrimp
along you,
breathing,
whenever
you want
to compose poems.

Marshall

It occurred to Marshall
that if he were a vegetable, he'd
be a bean. Not
one of your thin, stringy
green beans, or your

dry, marbly
Burlotti beans. No, he'd be
a broad bean,
a rich, nutritious,
meaningful bean

alert for advantages,
inquisitive with potatoes,
mixing with every kind
and condition of vegetable,
and a good friend

to meat and lager. Yes, he'd
leap from his huge
rough pod with a loud
popping sound
into the pot: always

in hot water
and out of it with a soft
heart inside
his horny carapace. He'd
carry the whole

world's hunger on
his broad shoulders, green
with best butter
or brown with gravy. And if
some starving Indian saw his

flesh bleeding
when the gas was turned on
or the knife went in
he'd accept the homage and prayers,
and become a god, and die like a man,

which, as things were, wasn't so easy.

The Soft World Sequence

I   *The Sea*

Through the glass floor,
from below,
he could see the girl
in the glass typing-chair,

in the glass skirt,
crossing her flesh legs
over the glass eye
in her groin. Glassily, it stared

at his own eye, and slowly,
the world of glass,
opening, closing,
became soft,

like the lips of an octopus
with eight legs
opening, closing,
in the Arctic ocean.

II   *The Clouds*

The man had been a bit
slow on the uptake, but
when his elbows went through
the light oak,

he saw the point. After his leg, too,
had sunk in

153

and was shivering
in the middle of the carbon-paper drawer, they began

to realize just how far
it had gone. Not even
the one in the telephone
bothered about the screaming then,

though it did make a hell
or a noise. It was how
to profit from it that occupied
all their minds. After so long

without anyone wondering
how they felt about it all,
none of them was accustomed
to making much of an impact. So

even the one in the floor
let him run his legs through
for a while without
worrying. Of course,

the man did wade in diminishing
circles, evidently
grasping (albeit rather slowly)
just how soft the whole

thing had become. It took him
several minutes, though,
to appreciate the full reason
for the watery coolness.

When he did,
there was more noise. The one in the PAX phone

got quite a headache
in its ear-piece.

Elsewhere I doubt
if they had so much trouble. Just
a fluffy moistness
easing in where

the old edges had been. And then
the slow, steady,
drumming, pita-pata
sound, as the rain started.

III   *The Earth*

Well, it was all, really,
a palpable jelly,
touchable, glaucous,
very good to eat

in its own way, if you liked
that sort of thing. I mean before
the day of the cucumbers.
After that, the hard edges

all became round heads,
and there wasn't much
you could do about it.
Not without risking

a hell of a row,
and maybe getting cut,
or swallowed up
in the ice. Let well alone,

I always say.
Take what comes.
You can't win them all. Not
without being one of them yourself.

Driving West

I

No, there was nothing first. Only his air
Stretching for ever, as it seemed. And wind
Cool on their dying faces from the hills
Where cars moved through dark forests, bearing gifts
And laughing children to the caves and mines
Far to the west. Where there was pine-scent, wheels
Hung in that air, turning each corner, stilled
On the brink of something.

              What was clear to see
Lay under lenses, burning in their dream
As they flew in. Bathed in such draughts of blue
As crowned his eyes, in clarity of means,
Awkward for nothing, they began the end
In even patience. And all followed, swift
As had been promised.

              Then, the summer lake
The war-lord wrote beside, his buttoned coat
Up to his neck, his long eyes evenly
Disposed, flung back the sun.

              To clapping hands
Each furled his flowered wings. And flowing rain

Came as before, and went, and washed them clean
Of all that blood-fall.

II

      Shielding his thin heart
He drove west as the day died: and the sun
Blazed in his face, clear dazzling like a brass
Cauldron to see the past in, or a gong
Booming with echoes.
       Life was thick with cars
Moving to meet the sea. That summer men
Spent the long draught of gold in going home
To what they loved, the shore. So when it came,
Darkness with all its visors down, it hurt
More than they knew. At first it seemed too bright
For anything but wonder.
         Low in the sky
The first blow was the blow of light: that night
Its crescent flowered in the east. It cut
Through glass of cars, through heavy walls of stone,
Through skull and fruit. And men like monks in cells,
Bowed on their knees, hands clasped behind their heads,
From zinc-lined solitude were shaken clear
And bathed in darkness. Miles of open light
Swallowed the naked and the lame. From this
No one walked through, and saw.
          The second blow,
After such radiance, was the blow of heat
As if an oven opened, or as if
An oven closed.
     The third blow was the blow
Of blackened wind. No frame of concrete stood
Near to the storm-boss unsplit. Blackened wind
Solid as iron was the mate of flame

157

And cooled the beaten anvils.
                              When it closed,
Then there was calm. Calm, and the ash. And while
The city rose towards red sky in the east,
Far westwards like an earthquake in the heart
It felt. Flung forwards by the blast, his head
Broke on the screen. Skin parted, and the blood
Moved in the shape of lightning.

                              Touched, with eyes
To see with, scarred, he saw. His clothes were stuck
To his back with sweat. Wet, shaking, he lay still,
Racing his head. Then one by one he moved
Ear, nose, lip, jaw, neck, waist, groin, knee, wrist, toe.
He was alive. He rose, then, pressing fists
Into what moved.

                              Miles down the road, past shreds
Of metal with their meat gone, gouged or stayed,
He saw the cans. Pumps fallen, petrol-smell
And air gushing from a gashed tube. *Here, then,*
He thought, *I can live here.* Heaped cans of oil
Shone below stars beside him.

                              So he turned
And fell head foremost to the gushing air
As the sun rose. And while it climbed in blue
He slept, marked with his blood.

                              And as he dreamed
Under the draught of air, his mind flowed out
And far down to the wells of darkness. Once
A short man with an axe beside a stream
Butchered a calf, and in the dream its heart
Fell on the grass, and crawled. Another time
Around a castle men who moved like pines
Grew to a noose that strangled. Old, asleep,
Washing slow hands in water, she was there,
Grey-haired and guilty, waiting for their thumbs

To choke her blood and stone.
                              Then he woke up,
Screaming: and, waking, head askew on cans
Of spilled oil, counting minutes, hearing wind
Sigh in the sunlight, knew that withering stone
Had caused her first death.

                              III

                    He drove back through blood,
Thinking of her. And as he drove things changed:
Noon-light to evening, there was nothing left,
Only a world of scrap. Dark metal bruised,
Flung soup of blood, anchors and driven screws:
The whole dead sea of wrecks lining the road
Emptied his mind. Ship after painted ship
Thrown into crumbs. He drove through nothing, dazed,
Awake, and dreaming.
                        Burning to the east
Where the city burst and scattered its fine seeds
Into the lap of air, the fires had died.
Only the veins, the main straight roads bored in,
Bordered by drifts of dust. Life thinned from stone
Through grit to powdered ash.
                              So he drove on,
Knowing his quest was meaningless and blank,
Towards what might have been. Then, by a curve
Where the road narrowed, as it should have done,
He parked the car, got out, and went on foot
To where she might have died.
                              There was no sign
Of even iron or fireclay. Stooping down,
He reached out his right hand to brush the dust
And part some, delicately, where she used
To part his hair. As if in sand he stroked

159

The shape of something in the dust, some shape,
And touched his eyes.

                Then he stood up, and took
A new coin from his pocket. With his heel
He dug a flat hole, flung it in, and scraped
The ash back over it, speaking aloud,
Or meaning to, these words: *where we lived first,*
Below our window, when they changed the house,
Workmen found coins. They proved its date, showed pride
Of earlier workmen for their blood-fall. Here
I show the same, where there is nothing. Only
The ceremony remains.

                And then he drove
Out of the dust-bowl, and across the plain
Back towards his refuge, and his cans of oil,
All that the war had brought him, and forgot,
Or tried to for a little, what had died,
Having done all he could.

IV

                Then, as before
That spear-flash in the evening, most were sick
And needed blood, knowing they all were doomed
As she was.

            Awake under buckled steel,
After what lapse of hours she stirred and moved
Still in the tunnel. There was no more light,
No train movement. Somewhere a faucet dripped
Water, blood, water on stone. Inside her brain
The blood beat back.

               Fire was the sign of blood.
After the first blow it returned and beat
Over and over at those broken doors.
It oozed from coal trucks in a rush of blue-

gold, yellow as gas here, mustard-sharp.
They smelt it coming. Acrid hint of smoke
Under carriage-cloth. Rake of hot-iron heat
Flaring on cheeks. And then that fast-back lick
Of its long tongue, flickering through each crack
In plastered skin and bone, liquid like knives
Cutting and salting. Wincing in its wounds
The whole train split like stitches.

                                  Men fought with tins
For knives to open tins. Bone-wounds from strikes
In the long club-war of survival healed
And left them hobbling. Over all that fire
Waiting to burst its banks and bleed them dry
They crouched like hens.

                        There leather creased and wore
Around low shoulders that were scarred with hawks
From earlier wars. Where in the wall men burned
For being nothing, thunder and leaves were borne
With songs of triumph. Wrenched from these, and oiled
In coats of black too seared with flame to cool,
Some walked and ruled. Walked when the last cars broke
And there was no more fire. In wars for this,
And pride, over the brick-waste they patrolled,
Circling like rooks. And when they found, they killed:
Or cured what insolence was left, ingrained
From scoured-out power, in pain.

                           Stumbling on rails
Towards that ring of sun, past sweating walls,
Or in her mind, as he had done, she moved
To that church, where she was due.

v

                           There by the grave
Beside slow falling clay she stood in dirt
And watched their heavy faces. Brass and lead

161

Had stamped their moulds in blue eyes and in brown
Before it happened. Under bells that speared
The cold larks in the clouds, the feuding clans
Blackened the day with grieving.
                            Far away
She saw the cows come downhill to cold farms
And feed on warm hay. Breathless, she recalled
A tight sow with her farrow in her skin
Scraping a nest of sticks for him to fall
And come alive in.
                  Waxed clay into clay,
The passage was performed. The oiled ropes ran
Under and over. And bronzed lion-masks
Amazed the worms.
                  Men coughed and stamped. And bones
Long bearing stress of birth were spared and fell
Into the space below the world they penned
Her glassy eyes in.
                In earth, in wood and stone,
The coffin-shape lay where it rested. One
Bowed in his hands, tears falling. Hard as ice
He was a winter cave where water flowed
Through aeons of slow time. The other stood
Seeing the keels beach in a sea-weed blaze
Along the western shore-line.
                        Layer on layer
The dwindling pyramid of the dead bled in
Over their faces. Red with heat of kin
After the cold earth, by the common grave,
They saw it coming.
                 Beyond her wrecked train
Outside that warring town she felt the chill
Take hold of her.
             That history of men
Marching with axes over these bared fields

Heraldic now at mid-day, mailed her brain
In heavy chains.
                        She sniffed, and felt hard rot
Smeared like an ointment, strangely thick and sour
Against her skin, ash-breath of coming death
Among the old. Old as they all were old
And he would soon be.

VI

                        Up the mourning stairs
All the white dogs turned round their eyes and frowned
As he came on. The cases creaked and stirred
With what was in them. Silence of clear glass
Behind which all the world could hold its breath
Until the moment came to scream, shivered
And knew its hour.
                        Holding that corpse in mind
The hall was taut with waiting.
                        Then blood broke
Over each surface it had oiled before
In even violence. Absolving red,
Crackling with iron spikes, it struck and spilled,
Swilling jet-metal. Cold wood shook and peeled
Under such pressures that the whole house bulged
Like a bag of water. Willy-nilly, walls oozed
Thick drops, then, blotched with patches, bleached
One even red. What was a refuge once
Wilted to a grave.
                        That night for the first time
Under one roof, sheltering from their grief
With port and ham, the cousins met. Like a dog
Blood ran between them with its nose to the ground
Sniffing for a scent. One slapped his covered sides
With a brace of gloves like a killed pheasant. One

163

Hunched his dead side, slurring his vowels like
A load of stone. What there was left to say
Under that flood of grieving no one knew
Except through money. Making, moved by, coins:
This was their only link. Hands shook that shook
Each other's hands. One with his stomach-wound
From alcohol, one rigid from the stroke
Of what had struck him as a child. Each merged
With the sores of Nature.

                  Outside, through blood, the kilns
Burned in the distance, and the bricks were fired,
Squared moulds for men, each holed with a dish. Men stoked
The rain-slaked furnaces with coke. Men scarred
Ledgers with ink. These were the fields of war
Where lines of men, black figures, marched and fell
Into the red of death. Hungry or old,
Some lay beneath bricked urns they built and sold
Miles from the houses they put up and bought
All beside slag, soot sifting down through clouds
Of massed rain.

            And that night the eastern ash
Gathered and swayed them to the gulf of war
Where all were game-soup. So the cousins met
Behind the kilns, under that night of blood,
Dying, and proud. And no-one spoke, or knew
How they could speak.

              Her father sat alive,
Dreaming of horses. It could come again,
Come once, and still his guts, they said, would hold
For a year and a day. If he could smoke and play
The bricks could scatter. There were colours, odds
Of another win. So he lay back in tweeds
Beside her cairn, drinking his wine. *Here, then,
Here's something for you, here*, he said.

                   Then blood

164

Broke in her dream, as dams break in the brain
To flood the cells. She dreamed of men and guns,
Keys jangling in a tiled hall, and a race
For broken glass. And then it all began
To merge in dazzling anguish of hot lights
Gashing the dark, gushing on walls.
                                    Coughing,
Tossing on red sheets, weeping in her dream,
She knew the end was near. She touched her hair
And felt grey rain turn into hail, white snow,
And cried for him.

VII

                    And as he drove he heard,
And stopped the car, and came to where she was,
Far in, still in the tunnel, blocked, alive
Behind her shattered glass. Her locked hands moved
Like brooched snakes round a cup. There cold red wine
Swirled like his blood. Her burned legs spread, she looked
Ready for death. He kissed her, touched her arms
Gashed to the wrists with red. Her knitted scars
Wove them a skin.
                    Far east the city fell
Into itself. Welded in white heat, fused
Under that hanging sword, they grew as one,
Her cold pearl coming to his shell-bred hands
In milk and scent of musk.
                            That second night,
Sleeping with her, he dreamed his father came
And frowned above him. Wearing black and mud,
He drew high pillars. Coal burned in his eyes
And beams collapsing choked him. Wind and sea
Broke through the hall they talked in, till they drowned
In flowers. Clematis, dark spider, touched

165

His cold face with her seven hands. He smiled
In his own garden once again. She moved,
His mother, shearing blooms. He was a child,
Married and dying in his mother's arms
Far from the war.
                    And then at noon he woke
With her dead in his arms. She who had lived
Yards from the blast, though miles beyond the blaze,
Dazed with the air had sickened. And so he
Lifted her up, and held her in his hands,
Her black hair falling.
                    Then his walk began
Back to the light-ring and the drifting ash
That would drown him soon, too. Toiling on rails,
Cracked up, he reached the pocked air. Hard and thin
His new breath came. He turned. And as the sun
Sank in the sky, he felt the poison stir
And knew the end was near. Starting his car
He drove on west, the ash-light in his eyes
Glazing the skin with gold. As in his grave,
Wearing his death mask, he moved into dark
Behind the wheel.
                    And as he drove he seemed
To wake and dream. Two knights lifted their swords,
One with a hawk on his left hand. His feet
Sloughed the rough dust as though on skis in snow
Near to his mountains in the east. Across
That blazing sea, beside his level bay
From which the coarse earth rises, the long port
Waited for his return.
                    And the other came
Short-necked and dark-haired, who had burned his palm
With a slow match. And looking to the light
Above the chair he lay in, stared and slept,
Though waking, to resist the pain. These two

166

Moved in his dream as he drove on and felt
The poison stirring.

               So the sun went down
And the car moved on into the western dark
Nearer and nearer to the sea. Those cans
Of lost oil lay behind, missed long ago
Like her, and their slow burial of the blood,
In gathering black. He heard no horn, no drum,
Only the waves breaking towards the shore
His headlamps bored at. And the gentle ash,
Feather of pity, settled in the wind,
Swirling to fill the earth.

                     So he drove on,
Wading in blood. And, as before and since.
The crown was lifted, and he sank to sleep
In darkness.

VIII

           And so driving in his dream
He reached the last beach. And the waves washed in
Over the waste sand where no others were
Except his past. There with his wooden spade
And coloured pail he walked along the wall
Searching for where to build. And where the sea
Came to its highest mark below the road
He made her mausoleum.

                 The war of coins
Boiled to a cream of spume. Here all that blood
He bathed and came from soaked his grains with salt
And filled the shifting turrets.

                  Far away
Furled in their fresh cocoons the butterflies
That broke the city slept. And bowls of tea
Passing from hand to hand confirmed the signs

Moving in open pages, quaint and fine.
Their line continued. Pictures in the wind
Sailed into water.

       And on western sand
Where he was dying the sharp water leapt
And seethed over the moat, sinking away,
As his dark royal blood sank, through all time.

A Light in Winter

I

    She sat, legs gripping, eyes
Upturning, in the front row.

         As he spoke,
Reeling through Vitruvius, she was vague
And nagging in his back mind.

         Then she asked
Something, out-urging slurred words.

           Sharp
In their intending, he took in high boots,
Voice, twisted fingers.

        As he answered, she
Hooked like an anchor, dragging at his groin
And brain.

    It ended, and the audience clashed
Towards winter traffic.

       As they broke the street,
Rain-lashed, with black cars shining, she
Hunched in her cords, mauve, belted.

         Her wet hair

Framed the bark eyes, distended, shawled
In the mist of drug-light.

As wrecked wood, she dredged
Through tangling weeds, dense people.

He caught up,
Switched to her step, spoke to her sidelong face
Against the crowd.

Impulsive, as she watched him, he
Took her arm, urged her through a glass door, leaned
With her at a bar.

Used to nothing, she
Tested his knuckles, gripped at them, drank gin
Through smoke and darkness, dodging questions.

In
The taxi later, tongued in leather, lipped
As they rounded Hyde Park Corner, her
High legs eased, fingers opened.

As they rode
Against each other's bodies, briefly, he
Sensed her powered absence.

When she slouched out, near
Where she was living, with her number in
His calfskin book, he waved, once.

She strudged in,
Clenched in her coat, stiff, man-like.

When he wrote
Arranging meetings, she was ill
And couldn't see him.

When she wrote back, he
Watched the blue, sick strokes wrangle on the page,
Sexed, wild.

As the need to see her fixed him tighter, he
Forgot his wife, job, only saw hard lust
Forged in a pouch for spending.

As he sketched

169

Through polished silence, or ate breakfast, poised
In jangling talk, he trembled.
                              In his bed,
Beside the jewel of his calm, his wife,
He felt an absorbed wilting.
                              So she came,
Flown from her darkness to his light.

II

                              At the place
Agreed, and in the time, oblivious to
His laid work, he sat waiting.
                              In his mind
The tower he was building dwindled.
                              When she knocked
Clutching a doll, in dark shades, barefoot, he
Shocked his firm nerves to ready taking.
                              By
The steel green cases, chilled, in half-dimmed space,
They kissed, holding.
                         In soft abandon, wrapped
Over a tautness of luxurious doubt,
Her mind enriched him.
                              So they came, hands held,
To a glowing room.
                         Men bowing, instruments
Of a bored thunder, lightened.
                              By the sheets
Of traced façades, pinned elevations, tricks
And fancies of irrelevant ornament, some
Shimmered in glass, charmed, winsome.
                                        Their
Willowy consorts, offered mistresses,

170

Pawed, shouldered, flouncing.
                              He
Faced them, detached, observed her.
                                   When she stood,
Silent, in others talking, her feet splayed,
Strange, goose-like.
                         In their eating, tumbling prawns
With a barbed fork, hot feeling found
Its symptoms.
                    They came out soon, cooled, and walked
To where she lived, hired attic.
                                       In bare lust
His teeth rattled, as a skull's.
                                    Her shift slid up
And over null bones, shielded.
                                     Muscular
And flexing, on that sewn quilt, she
Opened her purse of illness.
                                   As bent legs
Vaulted, spare arches into darkness, she
Enfranchised him in all she felt.
                                      So soothed
Into her world of subtle blurring, he
Straddled, half-dreaming.
                                Where her curved ways led
Him on, he walked in vigilant watching, ranged
Over her hills, through forests, by a stream
To the high castle.
                        In those crumbled foreign walls,
Echoing with bats and strange horns, he
Reached the jarl's table.
                               There he sat and ate,
Lifting the encrusted cup.
                                 And in his dream,
Swirled in an aura of sweet scents, he dived

Into a dream of dreams.

                         Lazily, whales
And sharks moved, reeling through green weeds,
Falling and killing.

                  When he woke, or lost both, they
Gasped in a sweat of cold, wind hissing in
Through an open window.

                       It was all
It never was.

III

               Low strangeness hung
Over his thoughts for long days.

                       She
Was in him, of him.

                  Under her thick spell
The arts of Christmas withered.

                    Her gloss card
With a black smile, some Negro, and her news
Of quarrels, mess, bored ailments, filled
His days with clear light.

                In exchange, his grooved
Whirling disc drove her furies back.

                   For hours
One night, that organ music ripped slick wings
To shreds.

         She moved in coolness to a cave
Where someone waited.

               Slow and cold,
Again those wings flicked.

                He was too far in
His own concerns to care, though.

               What she had
Was all the need of months for fullness, life

In the same room, a man's laugh.

                                      He could help

Only a little, less than he knew.

                                So she

Planned a disaster, helpless.

                            In the quick

Under the covers, even as they humped
Like spoons, in close liaison, it all soured
To a head.

                 One night she never came

At the known time.

                      Then later, they

Rang in the gross night.

                           She was back

With slit wrists in a locked room.

IV

                              As he read

The brutal card that told him, bolted in
A men's room cubicle, crude scalding drops
Melted the burned ink.

                     In his eyes

Her passion misted, emptied.

                       In dour grief

He folded what she sent, signed flowing letters, then
Graved them in memory, flushed them.

                         As he sat

Again beside that high glass, turning lead
In his poised fingers, he could see her arms,
Gashed, scarred.

                 In the watched room,

She crouched against the wall.

                       On a mattress, rigid

In locked fear, she spent hours.
                        The words rose back
Out of the blue square, swollen, blurred,
Thrashing his calm.
                    Day after day
Caged in that lift, as in his own taut mind,
He rose up, tried to see her.
                            She was tired
And seeing no one.
                    In four weeks she wrote once
In sprawled mauve, Japanese felt pen.
                                Illegible signs,
Frail, spidery.
                He read them, wrote back, hauled
Into a pitiable chaos of longing.
                                Gorged
On dreams of flesh and spending, he
Showed his remoteness.
                        In drab hints
Noted, and swallowed, his wife grasped, and hoped,
Still, it was office trouble.
                            On the screen
Others played out their drama.
                            Here it swayed
As a slow weight.
                    In thin poise, to and fro,
Their union clicked and held,
Saturate with the oils of mercy.
                                If
Her mind risked thinking he was faithless, she
Jibbed at the huge truth.
                        Soon
Their bodies would resume.
                            And so the year
Edged to the raw spring.

V

There, one iron day
She came out.
In the woods and galleries
He watched her grow back.
With her blooded arms
Under his own, he reached for softer passion, touched
Her delicate centre.
Where before, their minds
Fused in a drenched rush, now
They scorched in milder fire.
At Putney once
They strolled in prickling sunlight, spitting pips
Of grapes in the river.
Tanned by inward light,
Her pitted face, pinched by the winter heat,
Faltered in smiling, as they paused.
By an oak,
Racked into hollow fretwork, she stretched up
And kissed his neck.
He touched her razored arms,
Grown to the tree's heart.
So their pact was sealed
In hungry April.
How the sadder change occurred,
And moved the cured lust from the tender love
Into excess of dullth, he never knew,
Or faced.
For her perhaps the nub
Of change was in the stars, or in her blood,
Still blending, as do oils.
However it
Happened, it did so.
As the year burned, all

175

Settled, as on an isled sea.
                        Stretching to
Some edge of merging, their horizon calm
Of easy loving fooled both.
                        If she fretted, he
Bathed in a sweet lagoon of touching, gulfed
In swathing lust.
                  She grew remote, unpurged,
Ill at ease.
            Each night, when he rose, dressed
And left her in the low hours, edged with fear,
She felt resentment.
                    That first need
For someone sane receded.
                        In her healed
Half-grown new mind, a drive came for a friend
Less normal, wilder.
                    What she needed now
Was someone like herself.
                        Some final test
Of mended fibre.
                So the other, when he came
In burned late August, was
Inevitable, a laboratory.

VI

                    They had both
Gone to a stadium.
                    In her sheen of PVC
And plastic visor, she was modern, hip
And cured.
            As an attractive decoy, she
Lolled with her legs up.
                        Hinting boredom, by

176

Her shaken hair, she caught eyes.
                                Under the dome
In hectic arc-light, they engaged.
                                White cars
Raced in the stench of violent action, wrenched
Round and round a firm track.
                                He sat
Locking cold numbers on a board.
                                As each
Ripped and performed, he clocked them.
                                A man leaned
In easy leather, awkward, shy,
Offering her a cigarette.
                        In the glare
Of all those egos, flowered silk and sound,
He was relaxed.
                    She talked
Into his ear, laughed, strained with words
On the board.
            For Christ's sake take me home
And screw me, man.
                            He stayed with numbers, times,
Not caring.
                So the paired scales hitched and slid,
Upsetting them.
                    As iron, she withdrew,
Freed from the lodestone.
                            As he went to wash,
Leaving his metal case with her, she clutched
His arm, pleaded, said not now.
                                So he went
And came back with her gone.
                                So many times
In later weeks he was to feel the same,
This jealous bile, frustrated anger, hate

177

For a man's hair.
     That first night, shivering,
He drove home.
     In the bedroom, in the dark,
Undressing softly, he heard his wife breathe
In uneasy sleep.
     Not noticing, deaf
In his pain, he crept in, tried to join her.
        Crushed
In still hate, he sank under.
      Turning, he splayed flat
On his belly, slewing rucked sheets.
      In the heat,
Squalid with rumpled, anxious dreams, he heard
Rain, ramming the roof.
     Outside, thin birds
With breaking feathers, lifted, hurled
Oceans of muscle into bald air.
     As it burst
Through violence of pent wind, each was culled
Into a winnowing of silence.
     Furrowed earth
Eased with its worms.
    Black slugs lurched under leaves
Rustling huge drops off.
    As he lay, he felt
Raw tension settle into troubled shaking, pin
Stiff nerve-ends.
    Quivering, stilled,
He urged hot lips against the head-board.
      His wife turned
Out of some dream, half-crying, rising, lapsed
Once again, as a fish would, swept
In the down-draught, to the bottom.
     Then he slept,

Not meaning to, but tired.

                         And the storm rolled
All night.

VII

        In the morning, he rose, drove
To the tower site, over wet roads.

                    When he rang,
She sounded strange, numb.

               In the glass box
Over his papers, he was trembling, taut
As he fixed a meeting.

            Under the crane,
Watching the rubble swung, he saw her face
Teeming with dark fish, all day.

               Tense, at eight,
He collected her, raced through the savage park
To a lonely place.

           Against the wheel,
Pressing his head, he rested.

              With her knees
Locked back, hair swung off, hands clawed, she
Groped in her pain to help him.

              As the cars
Rocked past in flooding summer, singed with leaves
Out of the failing light, he saw the hands
Grip in the clock, stir, threaten.

              As the sour
Injustice hit him, he heaved up, surged, struck
Her bare face, forced his whickering hand
Against her clasped legs.

         In the untidy riot of clutched
Struggle in awkward space, clenched, hurt
And screaming, they scracked over chromium, glass,

179

Wood, stewed
In a hash of envious violence.
                           Then half-spilled
Through stupid angles, postures of abused
Self-hatred, they felt sex lift, steal
Into the crannies of cramped anger.
                               Leaning, strained
Over the leatherette arm-rest, they bunched up
In one seat, forged a broached umbrella, crammed
Each other.
              When the tumbled rush had passed
In white flights to the far horizon, they
Broke into two, lay over.
                 All
Mended for moments, it was closeness in
Their globe.
               His pride secured, he rode
Into the pleasure of remembered hope,
Forgave, and laughed.
                  She kissed him, and the stars
Crept into fresh positions, crouched for war
And evacuation.
             They drove back
In each other's arms, knowing the falls was near
And would overwhelm them.
                That was the last night
They even touched.

VIII

           Far away, calm at home
In a mews yard in Hampstead, hard
In grease-pocked overalls, the blond boy worked
Racing in neutral.
           Beside his door, high gloss

Shone on a bared, smear engine, moving parts
With inexorable power.

                       His oil-stained hands,
Uneven ways, washed straw hair, drew
Her into promises, cracked vows.

                       As he
Sketched late, at the point block, waiting, she
Never arrived, though swearing to.

                       One time
He took it, smiled.

                       The next, he felt hate stir
And thin despair flick.

                       So the autumn drained
Into a vacuum of envy, knowing love
Grate in its last few grains.

                       One evening, working late
Under the painful strip-lights, he
Dreamed in a waking terror.

                       He had gone
To see her, found them both there.

                       They were lax
After love-making.

                       When he came in, they
Woke, and then giggled, flaunting their bare skin,
Erect and goose-fleshed in his hampered face,
Famished with jealousy.

                       So he would seize
And work with scissors, hacking at their forks
With accurate hands.

                       Watch blood spurt, laughter split
Into a tattered agony of pleading.

                       Stop,
For God's sake, stop.

                       Then he found his calipers
Driven by white knuckles deep into the board,

And his arm shaking.
                    He unclenched his fist,
Striving to soothe himself.

IX

                    And then,
With no perceptible crisis, while
The chestnut walls burst open, and green mines
Exploded mahogany on gravel, he
Felt a control come.
                    Gradually at first,
Then tauter, with a sense of joy in things,
Love swivelled.
                    In his panelled house,
Dulled with the sound of ghostly breathing, all
The brooches pricked and held still.
                                        He was lulled
Through grown content, rich pleasures.
                                        As enwombed,
He lolled in safety, fed and sure.
                                His wife,
Salt in a hunger of envenoming tears,
Gathered, using her precious gains.
                                As she served
Him toast in a silver dish, hot soup, and kidneys, he
Grew to the will to love her.
                            Once again,
He saw the clean grace in her nose line, sweep
Of corn-grey hair, and clean clothes.
                                    As she bent
To lift a fallen paper, pain
At so much deceit of such a sure friend sucked
Hot sobs in his throat.
                        He remembered how,

Years back, another veering ended.

                                      In
The flare of trombones it began, with fears
Of marriage breaking, then
A drying started.

                   How, he never knew,
Or couldn't think now, only that it did,
And spread until they parted.

                           After weeks,
They nudged once, in a fruit shop.

                           Meeting her
Over those balls, Corbusier ovals, shapes
And odours of ground, sumptuous plenty, he
Dried like a thrown pip.

                   If love winced in then,
It could now.

               And this woman, with
The dove's hair, bird of passage, tamed and swollen, could
Be where it aimed.

                 As he watched her body sway
In sinuous elegance, a buried lust
Shivered, he touched her.

                     Tangled in their bed,
Under the skeins of tension, wet and sleek
In oils of passion, they could swim,
Each thought, in brine of pity.

                 So,
As always, in the need to last, alive
In friendship, each accepted what there was,
And used it honestly.

               He turned, and waved
In his mind, to the past.

               In the office, when,
Days later, truth rang, he was filing.

                   As

He set the bakelite back in
Its holder, he reflected how it seemed
So small, all bad news.
                              They
Had flown to France.
                              And so it ended, in
One sentence.
                    Why it had to, and why then,
He never knew, though knowing.

                              X

                              Looking out, through
That high glass, lashed with chill sleet, he
Slipped into winter, losing her.
                              Now she
Was all one with the shed seeds, fallen in
Some drift of snow.
                              Drumming the black shell
In its cradle, he began to sketch, eyes blind
With final hail, against the pain-storm.
                              Fined
Into a second of thin terror, he
Severed it all in flared lines, flowing shapes.
Showing her, what she was.
                              Was there so much
He never knew, in madness?
                              Now,
Under the axe, it seemed so.
                              As he sketched
Blindly, the tower of a stone church, high
On a precipice, overlooking a long drop,
He saw her coming.
                              As a black, slight figure, dots
Only, in one far corner, she

Mounted a path towards the light.
                                            A cross
Blazed, with a slung fish on the steeple, Christ
In seaward glory.
                          To that reach of salt and calm,
Lifting a black weight out of nowhere, she
Drove like a lost ship.
                                    Fighting, dying now,
Into a fluxion of tense water, calmed
And still, Narcissus, she was gone.
                                                    Then the door
Opened, and his wife entered.
                                            He tore off
The whole sheet, ripped it hard across,
Crunched it in the wastebin.
                                        He was back
In the plain present.
                              Once again
The ram broke, and across the window sleet
Swept as before, draining the light.
                                              He rose
And took his brief-case, and went home with her,
In a dream of children, running to kiss his hands.

The Bamboo Nightingale

a funeral song to America, for her Negro dead in Vietnam

I rise like a wooden bird from China. I sing
    from the echoing bellies of coolies

185

in the rice fields. I mount on a curved gable
  in South Vietnam. I scream
across the Pacific to where you bask with your dolphins

in the riches of San Francisco. All down the coast
  your Golden Gate opens
to the poverty of Asia. I speak to the oranges
  rotting on trees. I address
the Bikini-strip of Sausalito, the beats

poising their chop-sticks. I make you the music
  of hunger and blood
crying for redress. America, listen. You have raided
  the inarticulate one time
too many. The reckoning comes. Below the pagodas

moulded in rain, your GI boots fill
  with the feet of centipedes. Your cowboy
politicians march on their stomachs into
  the supermarkets of mercy
without their credit cards. Your dandy aviator

posturing in leather gloves at his microphone
  inverts his torch each night
at the Hollywood Bowl of money. His witches' Sabbath
  sieg heils. And your army
of drafted ex-slaves fights out and across the ant-ridden

basin of the Mekong Delta watched over by the wings
  of helicopters. Out-generalled
by the Granddaughters of the Revolution, they die
  for the inalienable right
to six feet of Republican ground. At Forest Lawns

186

the suicide fringe of your Upper Four Hundred are laid
    to rest in velvet. Your war
heroes are buried in a field commuters pack
    their abandoned Buicks by
a mile from the Pentagon. A shrouded crucifix

exploits the Passion. Each apache heart
    has a stake in it, the Old Glory
catches the throat. I see your packed quiver
    of machine-stitched chevrons, the
Redwood aisles are your coffin timber. It is

the apocalypse of unequal rights. I hover
    with the eye of a newsreel camera
above the cortège of a black sergeant. My zoom
    lens pulls up his mother's
creased face into sweating ebony satin for

your moment of truth in *Life*. I caption her: *Jesus,*
    my boy was a white man
the day the reds nailed him. Remember that war
    when the limbs of your KIA airmen
formed up by fours again from their cold storage

in a Normandy abattoir. The Oxford hands
    reverently placed them back
in their air-cooled coffins, caring only what colour
    they were. America, here
The checkerboard squares of your white dream intermingle

in aerosol incense. Your soda-fountains are a-glitter
    with the nickel panoply
of the plastic Christian soldier. Even his screams
    are canned. You embark for crusades
against the marijuana-culture your fifth

column of Shanghai laundrymen in Buffalo
        smuggles in across the Great
Lakes. It is war to the needle against the yellow
        men the black men
are impressed to be targets for. The splinters of *Lightnings*

rust in the bones of North Korean villages
        nobody bombed except with
propaganda. Oh, exploding paper hurts
        only the graduate squaw
with her head in the schizophrenia of *Newsweek*. Truncheons

of Crazy Foam ooze from their cylinders
        in the All-white wigwams at Culver
City. Where is the doped brave with his hand
        burned in the embers of a New
Deal? The traffic cops in Alabama

bite on the bullet. Amphetamine is the mother
        of invention. Oh, come on,
America. The old con won't work
        any more. In the high-rise
incinerators of Austin Confessional Verse

can snipe itself to a Jewish cinder. Cry
        all the way to the bank while we cool
the Capone generation. The B-feature
        illusion is over. Your gangsters
have moved to the groin. Tonight is the massacre

in the under-trunk of clover leaves, the St Valentine's
        Day of the mobile gasoline
war. Vanzetti dies in the punctured sperm
        of your golden-armour-plated
Cadillacs. America, I smell your orgasms

in the copper exhausts of Mustangs. I taste your burned
    flesh in the sassy-flavour
of breakfast foods on W U O M. Your hypodermics
    have entered the marble temples
of Lincoln. In the scrapyards of Arlington

the Galaxie and the Continental are one
    tin. Its canisters
have unfolded their soup of blood in the clenched knuckles
    of the hard shoulder. Dip
your wheel into vomit, America. Spoon into flesh, the

cornflakes of Minnesota are deaf to the crackle
    of burning skin. I give you
the toast of Napalm. America, wring
    the brass neck of your melting-
pot. Hanoi is the cauldron of truth. Saigon is

the blazing Southern Cross of the Isolationist
    paradise. Ky is the killer
the Carl Sandburg village has no room
    in its penthouse for. America,
listen. The Goldwaterism that shelters your cold

executives in their minds of Samsonite
    has filtered the sun to a trickle
of ashes in light. Their mouths gape and scream
    for clay. Between them your body
they care about less than the clear glass in their eyes

is drained like a horse to make veal. Where now has the fury
    of dried blood gone? ask
the Macarthurite bronze gods in the fought-over beaches
    of conquered Iwojima
decorated by the sea. In the grey heart

of the University Section the heirs of Walt
    Whitman are a mile high
on the morning glory seeds of electrodes clipped
    to the genitals. The great
American epic rocks in the spilled bowels

of Dillinger. The internal war game
    of mah-jong continues
by the yolk of human eyes. The monks burn
    into silence. There is no one to sweeten
the acid policy in the porcelain

of your LBJ Acropolis. Call it the Black
    House, if you like. It looks
that way to the dark sergeant whose brains were charred
    with the legacy in the headlines
of the *Times of Pecayune*. His eyes are closed

to the peacock of the American rainbow. His ears are deaf
    to the buzzing of W A S P S. His nose
is open to the stench of rotting corpses rising
    out of the jungles of Hanoi
to corrupt the affluent. His mouth is twisted

with the sour flavour of black blood. His hands
    are burned like an eskimo's
with the ice of not minding his business. America,
    listen. This is the end
of the everlasting Charleston, the Wall Street crash

on the dollar merry-go-round, the dime hand-shake
    in the golden soup-kitchens
of disillusion. I weep for the onion-domes
    of the Kremlin. This is the bite
of iron. If you forget it your millionaires

will die in their X K Es for a brass thimble
    of Curaçao. The days
of the sugar economy are over. The guerrillas walk down
    your skyscrapers, beating
their steel breasts for the oiled virginskins

of Los Angeles. America, listen. Your body
    moves like a moth in the beautiful
stage of emerging from metal. Her chrysalis
    is the scrap-tide of iron. You advance
minute by minute towards the wheeled oblivion

of the killing-bottle. Take off your leopard-spot coat
    and bathe in the Yangtze river
with me tonight. There is no one to judge our battle
    except the future. I ask
for a striptease of guns. Lay aside your helmet and swim

for an hour in the moonlight. Perhaps beneath the willows
    in the evening cool of the water
some peaceful magic will happen. I ask you to move
    into the fluid of reason
below the lianas. I wait to bathe you in oil

or in blood. Answer me out of your prosperous iron
    in San Diego. Address
some message of sorrow to me in Saigon. Send
    your Pacific troubled with waves
of Oregon pity. Say that you hear and will come.

On the Thunersee

circa 1901

I

       Meanwhile, the Baron Albert
Emil Otto von Parpart
rose from the left side
of his brass bed
and walked (first drawing
the curtains embroidered with blue thistles)
to the window, which he opened.
               Stepping through
onto a stone parapet, he stretched,
naked, in the cool air.
          Across the lake
he could see the peak of Niesen,
above Spiez.
      It was a fine day.
      Turning,
he re-entered his bedroom.

II

         Meanwhile, his wife,
the Baroness Adelheid Sophie
Margaretta née von Bonstetten,
rose from the right side
of his brass bed,
which was also hers, and walked (first drawing
the curtains embroidered with blue thistles)
to her dressing room.
      There,
beneath a cylindrical, brass chandelier

fashioned with rosettes, she waited,
seated naked at her white dressing table,
until such time as the Baron should have washed.

(There was

only one bathroom.)

III

Meanwhile, the Baron,
having greeted the day, proceeded
to the glory of his ablutions.

Passing
through the first of several mahogany doors, he arrived
almost a little breathless,
on the upper level of his bathroom.

There he settled,
with some ceremony, his naked buttocks
on the lowered oak
of his English water closet.

Evacuating
at his bare ease, the detritus of the evening's brilliance
into clear water, he rose
(as Christ) a second time, and flushed
what was left of himself
to the lake of Thun.

Through a linked series
of ingenious pipes, it fell
down forty feet of landscaped elegance
to amaze the perch.

IV

Meanwhile, the Baron,
unmindful of these metallic services,
bent down
to the sheet steel

of his hip bath.
                    Kneeling in this,
as to the pew in their chapel his ancestors,
he absolved himself
with much grunting, and a little exercise,
of the body's dirt,
which is the sins of the flesh.
                         So cleansed,
upright at the mirror
above the hand basin, in a white bath-robe,
the Baron shaved.
                    A little blood
flecked the marble
as he picked off some alert prominence
in the noble chin.
                    He dabbed
at the shorn skin.

                         v

            Meanwhile, his wife,
having thought over the day's impressing obligations,
containing her luxuriant wastes, as best she might,
on plaited cane,
grew restive.
            He was longer than usual.
                                   She
sulked.

                         vi

       Meanwhile, the Baron,
having freed the temple of his deserts, the body,
of the night's adhesions,
descended to the second level

of his bathroom.
                    Throwing aside the bathrobe,
he began the slow process
of powdering himself.
                    Thereafter,
again naked,
he strode to his dressing room.
                              On the glass-topped table,
beside his riding boots,
a manual of Gymnastic Exercises lay open.
                              He tugged
the tasselled bell-pull in the doorway
to inform his wife
her way was clear.
                    With a sigh, she moved,
at some speed, and in perfumed openness,
to the seat of her relief.

VII

                    Meanwhile, the Baron
(I draw a veil
over his wife's commensurate exertions, she was
no longer young)
extended his frame
in the morning lists of health.
                    So flushed
and bronzed, steeped
in a warm glow of remembered muscularity,
the Baron dressed.
                    As was his custom,
selecting without warrant of valet or chambermaids
the minimal tweeds
for the day's toilings, he hummed

195

a few bars of *La Bohème*, as he moved
between press and dressing table.

VIII

        Meanwhile, his wife,
now washed, and restored
to some fine ghost
of her former splendid narrowness, withdrew,
once more, to her dressing room.
        Whether maids,
masseurs, or her own mere sleight of hand,
had achieved such miracles as had been achieved,
discretion conceals.
      In her clothes,
thrown on with care, though quickly,
she presented a firm spectacle.

IX

        Meanwhile, the Baron,
returning in waxed magnificence
for the day's affrays,
humming and calm
passed through the curtains
embroidered with blue thistles.
        Admiring his wife,
he kissed her.
      Turning, he then strode,
with some purpose, and in high fettle,
along the mahogany corridor
towards the landing.
       To his left he nodded
to his first Mucha,
a girl clothed, who drew

196

the sheet up to her coy neck.
                         To his right
he winked at his second Mucha,
a girl naked, who drew
the sheet down to her wanton waist.
                              He felt
peckish.

                    x

           Meanwhile, before him,
his double stairway with the wrought-iron flowers,
and the lamp standards,
plunged like the Trummelbach Falls through its naked rock
towards the smell of kippers.
                    The Baron descended,
as do the angels, even, sometimes,
to the satisfaction of the fleshly appetites.
                              On the shell terrace,
in the sound of falling water,
the Baron attended, opening his letters
with an ivory paper-knife,
to all intents and purposes amused,
his wife's delayed arrival.
                         It was the year
of Jugendstil.
           A brooch by Lalique
drooped a florescence of contrived waterlilies
above his bending head.

                    XI

           Meanwhile, his wife,
already tapping the yew balustrade in some distemper
with her manicured nails,

was on her way to join him.
                              Knowing this,
and the minutiae of her habits to the last detail,
the Baron rose.
                    Ringing for breakfast,
he allowed the perfect Swiss clock of the world
to resume motion,
as it would continue to do,
without interruption,
for exactly thirteen years,
four months, and one day.
                              Knowing this, too, perhaps,
or having arranged it, as so many other things,
the Baron ate, without sparing,
cheese, rolls, marmalade, eggs, meat and honey-cake,
and, when he had finished,
wiped his mouth on his napkin,
belched, and, with a perfect conscience,
shot himself, through the brain.

                                  XII

                         Meanwhile, his wife,
the Baroness Adelheid Sophie
Margaretta née von Bonstetten,
having arrived, and eaten,
rose, and with a faint ruffle of her fastidious cuffs,
rang for the maid, who would, with some care,
clear the table.
                 It was a fine day.
                              She opened her letters.

To a Slow Drum

a stately music

I

Solitary thoughts,
and burial mounds,
begin this dirge,
and mournful sounds.

II

Now to the dead march
troop in twos,
the granite owls
with their *Who Was Who*s,
the bat, and the grave, yew
bear on his wheels,
Tuborg the pig
with his hard wood heels.

III

Gemmed with a dew
of morning tears,
the weeping armadillo
has brought his shears:
the droop-ear dog
and the lion come,
dipping their long waists
to meet the drum.

IV

On the bare chafing-dish
as each one hears,
the grey lead pigs
reverse their spears:
grooved in line,
they show no grief,
grouped above a sere
and yellow leaf,
a tree's life blown
through a crack in the door.

V

Over the red-black
kitchen floor,
Jeremy the spider
stalks to his place,
all eight legs
wet from the waste:
he climbed up the drain
to be here on time.

VI

Now, to the slow
egg-timer's chime,
shiny in state
come things from the grime:
tiny slaters
with wings and hoods,
beetles from the closet
under the stairs:
gashed with sorrow
each fixed eye stares.

VII

  Fairbanks crawls
from his winter leaves:
  he rubs his eyes
on his prickling sleeves:
  rattling his plate
for a sad sound,
  his black legs cover
the chill ground
  at a fair speed:
he creeps to our need.

VIII

  Now the hall resounds
to the tread of toes
  as each one gathers,
and the crowd grows:
  broken-spirited,
the bears upstairs
  troop to the banisters
and droop their ears:
  the brown one squats,
glum cheeks in his paws,
  the blue one strums
a melancholy string.

IX

  From all feasts of fish
we wove good fur:
  alas, no fish
stale death can deter.

X

As the drum beats,
the long cortège
winds to the attic
as towards the stage:
some hop and skip,
some crawl or run,
the sad music
holds every one:
crouched by the window
all weep to view
Peter, poor Peter,
drift up the flue.

XI

Now, all together
they chant his dirge,
grouped by the ledge
where the chimneys merge.

XII

Peter, salt Peter,
fish-eating cat,
feared by the blackbird,
stung by the gnat,
wooden-spider collector,
lean as a rat,
soon you shall fall
to a fine grey fat.

XIII

Peter, salt Peter,
drift into the wind,
enter the water

202

where all have sinned:
        forgive us our trespasses
as we forgive yours:
        remember us in heaven
as clean scales and furs,
        as we you on earth here
where any cat purrs.

XIV

        Peter, salt Peter,
farewell and live,
        as we do remembering
and so forgive.

XV

        Over the whole world
a sad pall falls,
        fur into fine air,
bone into ash:
        a chill water
wets every lash.

XVI

        Peter, salt Peter,
by pleurisy slain,
        the pale glass weeps
in its wooden pane,
        come to the cat-flap
and slap in again.

XVII

　　　Peter, salt Peter,
the bird of death,
　　　a boding raven
chokes off my breath.

XVIII

　　　Wrung warm tears,
and doleful words
　　　end this dirge,
and the screams of birds.

For the Arrival of a New Cat

The new cat is coming, is coming, the
green frog with glass eyes
　　is croaking. He squats
　　in the grate on his three legs in
　　　faience alertness. Beside him
the pot bear with
black eyes is lifting
　　his nosed head, he
　　　sniffs at the temperature, and
is ready. Outside in

　　the garden, the fuchsia is
ringing its red bells in
　　　Japanese pleasure. It
　　dangles its tongues in delight. The

spirea
flourishes plumage of pink which is
blue when
    you look at it closer. The new cat is
        coming, is coming, the
roses expect him. Upstairs, in

    the attic, the locked trunks are
creaking. Their papers and letters
        grip their teeth tightly. The
    new cat is coming, is coming, the
        books on their white shelves are
scattering leaves to receive him, their
spines are his servants. The
    carpet with purple pagodas is
        buffing its flat felt to
make him a warm bed. The new cat is

    coming, he moves with his
cone tail
        into the passage-way, over the wall, and,
    with tumbling abandon,
        down along bumpy and moss-filled stones to
the house he will live in. He
opens
    his new mouth and silently,
        almost silently.
screams a small welcome. The

    storm which has gathered is breaking, the
hotness expands and
        explodes in a fanfare of
    raining and thunder. Inside, by the window,
        the new cat is watching, is
watching. The new cat has come and

the storm is
   his celebration. With slit ears, he
      frowns through the glass which
is wet, and protects him. The

   new cat is coming, is coming, the weather
intones his arrival, it
      spells it with showers, and lightning
   flashes across four gardens to
      mix him a joy-song. He
turns on his back, and
rolls over and sleeps
   with his paw on his face. He is
      tired, the new cat
is tired, the new cat is sleeping.

   As he sleeps, he is dreaming, he
dreams of a rainbow. It
      burgeons, and flowers,
   fluttering petals of peonies, meat-red
      and pretty. The new cat
dives in his dream through a paradise
thick with the perfume
   of coley
      and raw steak. The new cat has
come to his house, he is happy.

A Poet's Life

The poet, today, is at home. His house, by a friend
    has been said to be 'crumbling, and graceful
    though small'. The poet loves it
and lives well. Might the casual passer-by catch him
    issuing forth from its doors
    with spade and hoe? Well, no,
the poet is no gardener. He prefers
the indoor life. By the fire one might see him reclining

on a white Indian carpet. Beside him, some books
    and perhaps a peppermint cream
    convey the mood. It is evening,
although the curtains remain undrawn, and the poet,
    as poets will, is obeying
    the urge to compose. He composes:
today I got up at eight, felt cold, shaved,
washed, had breakfast, and dressed. We observe him

sucking his pencil. He looks at his watch. It is eight
    o'clock. With a cough, he rises,
    propelling himself with an angular
swoop to the television set. Having pressed
    the appropriate button, he turns,
    returns, rearranges his legs,
and is ready. Tonight is *Avengers* night. As the screen
sounds and lightens, as screens will, the poet settles.

The poet is angry. On Thursday, while talking, he heard that
    his book had received some attention
    in the form of a notice in

one of the lesser-read weeklies. The poet, of course,
    was pleased when he saw the size
    and the title of it. To be
abused by the critics amused him. He scanned, with pleasure,
the offending phrases. His truth, he learned, was *transformed*

by fright wigs and plastic incisors (the poet reached out for
    his *Shorter Oxford*, thought better,
    and read on) *into the process-shot*
(whatever that was) *world of Bela Lugosi.*
    It sounded bestial. So the poet
    stares through his classical window
at a few amber chrysanthemums. In his barren garden
an overgrown pine steers up its feathery tail

to the pocked sky. An evacuating pigeon
    swings by the coconut-shell
    and coos. Having first felt pleased
the poet begins by imperceptible stages
    to feel less pleased. He watches
    the accumulating mound
of pigeon-shit. The poet selects a pencil. Laying
all wrath aside, he begins to write. In the dry,

prosaic, and somewhat indigestible mixture
    of decent feeling and sly
    wit he experiments
with, he commences his defence. I will not, he decides,
    give way to my self-indulgence.
    Never. Nevertheless,
in his fit of metre he nearly did. Well, nevertheless,
he enjoyed his poem, and grew less angry. Who wouldn't?

Tonight the poet is reading. He stands on wood
    in a bare hall. Before him
    some twenty or thirty young women
hunch over their desks and glower. The poet is something
    new. They have come to listen.
    They all, in their own way, write
and the poet, in his way, will show them how the professional
writes. A harsh overhead light glares. One shifts

with a hiss of tights. The poet observes, as he reads,
    a distracting world of thighs
    he would like to stroke. In his mind
he strokes the thighs. The young women, as women are,
    aware of him looking, reveal
    rather more than before. He reads
in a dubious mist of lust. Meanwhile, the mistress
glints through her spectacles, and is bright as a bird.

She is neither a bird nor a mistress. The room is cold
    and the poet heats his feet
    with a soft-shoe shuffle across
the barren boards. A girl titters. Her breasts
    under her wool sweater
    heave and invite. Encouraged,
the poet attempts a more comical poem. In his mind
an image of after the reading emerges. He strokes it.

Well, are you ready for questions? The spectacles glint
    as the plain ones parade their minds
    with a show of force. With a sigh
the poet sinks back. He deals with the questions. He gives
    what they need. He is charming and kind.
    He feels old. As the evening ends

with the usual round of applause, the poet retires,
refusing cocoa. He walks to his car in the rain.

IV

It is Saturday. The poet is shopping. Purposefully,
 he advances upon the town
 in green wranglers. All week
in his three-piece suit, at his wooden table, before
 his plate-glass window, the poet has
 chafed, he would have us believe,
in a rather too elderly image. Today, with his black
suède tie, and his creaseless trousers, he feels more relaxed.

He walks with a spring. He nods to a dog, as he strides
 to the door of the supermarket,
 swinging his flowered sack
from Heal's. There are dozens of young folk, swinging
 their flowered sacks from Heal's.
 The poet belongs. Toughly,
he swings through the doors as a man might swing to a bar
in an early 1940s Western. He plucks

a wire tray from the pile. Old women, amazed
 at this odd young man in the cords,
 shop on. The poet drives
towards the vegetables. He is Allen Ginsberg
 about to compose a poem
 featuring Walt Whitman. He selects
what he wants. Admired by babies and old men, he conquers
the meat counter, is beaten by eggs. With a weight

of the usual urban packages, he retreats
 to the queue. Like the others, he kicks
 his tray, and feels virtuous. These people

210

are all, as he is, in the process of living. They shop
    and are one. The poet is looking
    at life for his poems, is helping
his wife, is a normal considerate man. He feels calm
and at ease, as they pack his sack. With a fiver, he pays.

v

The poet feels grieved. He has been with his friend. She was
  ill
    and, as often before, not amused
    by the poet's talk. It is not
as if the poet has many friends. He would like,
    as so many poets, to seem
    more wild than he is. He is fond
of appearing a bit of a devil. However, at heart,
the poet is timid. Three times a week, he takes care,

and visits his friend. She is grateful. Of course, one's friends
    are delighted to see one. The poet's
    friend is delighted. Today
she was less delighted than usual, though. They went out
    to have tea, at their usual shop,
    in the rain. When the poet proposed
what was in his mind, she was unresponsive. Alas,
it can sometimes happen. The lady preferred to eat cake

than to shiver home in the wind and, in awkward haste,
    be coaxed in her chill room
    to perform a service. The poet
appreciated the point. He proposed that they leave
    at once, and without their tea,
    or even their cake. Alas,
it was not a wise suggestion. A cloud appeared
on the calm horizon. A rift appeared in the lute.

211

So the poet is in his bath. He is washing. He soaps,
    as do other men, with a slow
    and meditative motion,
reflecting. *I know I am right. I know*. The poet
    knows he is right. He soaps
    what he wanted her to have soaped.
He is irked by the thought, is enraged. He soaps,
and he thinks of her. He grows rigid. He whips her with soap.

VI

The basin is cold. The tap is cold. The wall
    sweats with cold. The poet
    is blind with suds, he is bent
over the bowl, he is dizzy and wet. He gropes
    for the sachet of egg-yolk. The sound
    of the slow-warming water is sullen, it
slubs in the basin with fretful reluctance. The sleeves
of the poet are unrolled and soaking. His shirt sticks

to his meagre sides. He is ruffling his locks in a grey,
    greasy malevolence. The
    poet pauses. His head is
shod in hot water. He muses. Is this the moment
    for a Zen awakening? *I wash,*
    the poet writes in his wet
head, *my hair. I am entered by Infinite Thoughts.*
Upright, though upside down, I am filled with freshness.

Wisely, the poet revises. Prone on the floor,
    he attempts a drier style
    as he dries. *My bushy head*
sprouts like a tree. In electric magnificence
    the poet feels like Keats
    or a Beatle. He dries and floats

in a hush of inspired musing. New lines emerge
from his sheltered life. He scraps them, and falls asleep.

VII

At last the poet has made it. The neighbours have bought
    his book on the war. In the room
    with the flock wall, and the nuts
on a silver maple, a drink of gin is on offer. He
    sips it, and smiles. His dentist
    here for a drink, too, smiles
with a knowing smile at his smile. He knows what it cost
the government. So the poet talks. Will he sign

his book? He will certainly sign his book. He signs
    with a deprecatory shrug
    an illegible note. They are asking
how he can manage when, after all, – Well, he does it
    mostly, he tells them, at night
    when the telephone can't ring
and you don't have to eat. They all gaze at the uneating poet
in his thin bones. How the Muse must nourish herself

on the empty air! The poet feels vaguely mocked
    through the maze of gin. He withdraws
    to a frowning seclusion. The talk
surges towards other topics. Like teeth. And Tolkien.
    The poet grits his teeth.
    He is miles away, in a wood
where men are kicking each other to death. As often,
urged by the social, he strays to the savage. He dreams

in a dull vapour. The guns thud. He leads his men
    over the top. The whistle
    gripped in his teeth, he advances

213

through German wire. All around the exploding shells
    destroy mere boys in attractive
    postures that war artists
can make romantic. The poet is not destroyed.
He gallops towards his medal, his battle-dress flecked

with a touch of distinguished blood. More gin is poured
    through the poet's dream. Half-roused,
    he sways to his feet. Are you going
so soon? The poet must reach Bapaume. He is making
    excuses, is threading his way through
    the trenches towards the door
in the whine of tracers. Outside, exploding flares
shower sad light. He dies back to life. He feels awful.

VIII

The poet is going abroad. He walks with the purposeful
    tread of James Bond
    towards the airport bus
which will carry him safe through the fog to his waiting wings.
    There they are gleaming. He stands
    admiring their silvery glow
on the grey tarmac. He steps to attain them, and slips
in a puddle. At speed, his fellow-passengers pass him.

Settling inside, he is stuck with a seat by the wing.
    Sighing, he fumbles, and fastens
    his seat-belt. He sucks,
as he always sucks in the air, an orange ju-jube.
    He is ready for anything. The
    engines cough. The wheels
turn. Accelerating towards its shattering roar,
the Boeing takes off, and tilts its nose in the air,

214

reminding the poet of cavalry charges. He leans
   back on the soft head-rest, a
   little high on his two
dramamine. So this is flying. The poet
   flies. He is in the air.
   He is high in the air
over England, above the clouds, on his way to work,
reading his poems to people abroad. He feels proud

to be famous, to be the poet. He stares through the glass
   at an Arctic sea of clouds
   dipped in the Oxford marmalade
of an English sun. So this is England. He feels
   like Kipling. Composing a hymn
   of praise to the shores he is leaving, he
drifts into half-sleep. *O England, I love thee,*
sailing on wings American over thy shores.

The poet sleeps, in a dream of stars, and stripes.
   Waking, he shakes himself.
   They are offering food. He reaches
to receive the beneficient tray. Gracious, he smiles
   at the capped woman worker
   who hands it to him. Her frown
drops him to earth. With a shrug, he assaults his chop,
his dry peach, and his cheese. He feels small, and alone.

IX

The poet has landed. He stands in Berlin. He is waiting
   for someone to pick him up. He
   expects a driver. He moulds
in his mind the image of who will drive him. It is
   a short, squat man
   of about fifty, wearing

215

a leather coat, and boots. He perhaps salutes.
The poet is doubtful. He censors the driver's salute.

The doors open with a soft, exiguous, rather
    sexual *thock*. The poet
    enters. The doors close.
He is lapped by the plush thighs of a black Mercedes,
    all noise deadened, all
    boring and trivial realities
excluded. His ex-Africa Corps chauffeur drives,
exuding competence through his Luger head.

Are you the professor? The poet starts from his thoughts.
    An irreverent boy with a grin
    and a wind-cheater confronts him.
He nods with a groan. His cases are carried, and stowed.
    He bumps along in the back
    seat of a badly sprung
Volkswagen bus. It grinds, with the windows open,
through a German wind. In the stench of petrol, he retches.

x

The poet is buying a cat. The cats glare
    from behind the tight wire
    which protects the poet from them. He
pokes his finger, gingerly, into one's ginger
    fur. It stirs, with a growl,
    like a dog. The poet withdraws,
uneasily nursing himself. He walks on to the purr
of a grey dollop of elephant-coloured ice cream

flounced on a blanket, and frowning. It stares at the poet
    as if he has just been emptied
    out of a tin. It doesn't

want to eat him. The poet attunes himself
    to the feline mood. He moves
    from cage to cage, growling
and frowning. He growls and frowns like a cat. *Can I*
help you? A face, the first he has seen with a smile

blocks his advance. The poet adjusts his growl
    to a cough. *No, thank you, I need*
    something a little smaller.
He needs a small cat. He would like a small, friendly cat.
    There are no small friendly cats.
    All purr, and are fierce. The poet
despairs of buying a cat. He edges towards
the emergency exit. Outside, a chained dog howls.

XI

The poet is in his office. Light through the blind
    is making pretty patterns
    across his type-writer
and his blonde secretary. The poet is pursing
    his lips in thought. His blonde
    secretary is pursing
her beady pencil. From other offices,
on either side, we hear the sound of laughter,

typing, and something on a tape recorder. The poet
    reflects a moment. The sun
    continues to filter through
the Venetian slats on the poet's toys. His trays
    froth with paper. His floor
    exudes a faint smell
of spilled coffee. The poet's attention strays.
His mind wanders. He dreams he is floating away

217

on a magic carpet of Turkish Delight to a harem
　　of blonde secretaries
　　to whom he dictates his slightest
whim. The poet composes an advert. WANTED:
　　GIRL WHO SEEKS INTERESTING
　　POSITION. SOME DICTATION. The
poet wakes, with a start. He resumes rejecting
where he left off. Rejecting, he feels rejected.

XII

Whoopee! He is in *Who's Who*. He leafs the pages
　　accounting for which of his friends
　　is still not in. He smiles,
observing with sad delight the absence of those
　　he is closest to. He frowns
　　to discover the presence of one
he has always seen as a rival. The poet sinks
into a reverie. He creates the ideal

Who's Who entry. He starts with a two-gun
　　salute like the one (he forgets
　　which) of the maharajahs, goes
on with Eton and Sandhurst, OM, CH,
　　etc., a medal for saving
　　life in the Persian Gulf
in 1922, and the best clubs:
Boodle's, Athenaeum. Recreations:

fishing, standing in rays of sunlight, malice. The
　　poet wakes with a jerk
　　from his dream. A page
with one he has always loathed affronts his eye. He
　　measures the length of the entry,
　　consults last year's, and finds

218

(horror of horrors!) the bastard was in then, too.
The poet closes his eyes. He swallows. *Who's Who*,

as far as he feels tonight, had better become
    Who Was Who, as soon as may be. He
    hoists its red weight
in his hand, allows it to flop, flat on its back
    on his coffee table. He feels
    annoyed to feel angry, though angry,
and rather let down by *Who's Who*. They ought to know better.
The poet frowns. He closes *Who's Who*, with distaste.

The Keats Odes Retold

1 To Autumn

      Well, darling,
      cock-teaser of
            old Mr
      Hot-pants
      with your fogged eyes, and
      breasty look,
            don't tell *me*
      you didn't plan
      the whole bit with him,
                plastering
      swags of bunchy
      grape-fists over the lintel,
                dipping
      shagged hawthorns with

gew-gaws,
             stuffing
au pairs with cream-cheese
et cetera,
                marrow-blowing,
nut-sucking,
                and generally
extravagantly exploding
nosegays
             under the velvet arses
of bum-boys,
                with a promise
it was all going
to keep on happening
                      hot and strong,
musk-knickered,
                   into the small
hours.

        OK,
we know who
was threshed
             in the elevator,
coming all the way from the intersol
to the viewing platform.
                         Also what
went on (or off)
that night behind the barn
in the stink of cow shit,
                     forked wide
for the queue in turtle-necks
after the May Ball.
                    I've heard
how cool you kept

220

the long plungers,
                    and those attentive
kitchen touches, draining
the beer-and-have-a-bash
boys.

        Of course,
I take your point. They don't
all want
            the tarty sprig
in her first sprinkle,
                    it's nice
once in a while
to get down
along the Embankment
                    with the shepherd's
delight raging,
                shaved and randy,
and flick the stiff midges
out of your eyes
                    beside the Needle,
gunning that sexy exhaust,
                        fetching off
the fresh chicks in the Wimpys,
eyeing straw blondes
                    in the clip joints
and the odd busty old pro
in Lyle Street
                from her top storey,
and then settling for you,
bitch-goddess,
                under
the club-lights
respectable, sexy,
                with a touch

of Rita Hayworth
a touch of mother and
a touch of Mata Hari
                              off to the south
soon for a winter
in bouncing Monte.

II To a Nightingale

All this flatulence, and
the pins and needles,
                              and then
to be turned off
like tipping *Harpic*
                              down
the *Humphrey*, well
it gets my goat. Oh I'm
not jealous,
                    Flutterby,
it's just I see you
cooking all our gooses
when you open
                         that
big mouth of yours.

      I need a *Pimm's*. Touch
of the old rabbit food
                              out
of the freezer, smell
of the gay Flamenco, and
                              those hot sands
on the Costa. Or maybe
a jar
      of West Country
draught, fizzing,

with steaks in it,
                        and then
the quick fade-out
into the bushes.

    Look, mate, you
don't know,
                what it's like:
crouched up all day long
over the in-trays
                        in the office:
bugged by rachitic
                        old bitches
and the starved look
of the Twiggys.
                        I just
throw up every time
I stop to notice
                what with
all that smudged mascara, and
the music stopping,
                        leaving
someone else stood up.

    Go on, I'll not
get stoned tonight.
                        Sex
in the head, though,
                        unknotting
opaque me
with gauze imaginings
as, e.g.
            the
toothsome cool

of Lady Midnight,
                        her bunch
of grapes in spangles,
bright fairies.
                   Yes, but
not here
in the dim smoke
                    of the green-room
on the soft carpets.

   Here, it's more
the womb touch, all
Voysey papers,
                   and a drip
of joss-sticks, with a hint
of the usual
                periodic
eccentricities: lichees,
green-sickness, and
                        prickling:
hemp and morning glory
seeds, with a few
                   well-drawn
puce groins by Rops,
not mentioning
                   those laid flagons
rich with cream
and hissed round
                   by the bar flies.

   You know
for years I've felt
I'd like to pack
                the whole
thing in, even

written out
            my famous
last words
about *melting*
into the world spirit
and so forth.
                What with,
you here
and it being all dim
                    and lively
I half-fancy
it for real.
            Just think,
to get hitched
with you in full flight
and me all comfortable
                        in
the alcove.
            It wouldn't work,
though.
            You'd soon turf
me out
        for dropping off
before your climax.

    Anyway, you were
never the settling-in
sort.
        You've been around
a long time, flier.
                    Out
at Billy Smart's or the Palace,
in by the bullrushes,
fluttering hearts with

lashes,
        always
the open-eyed chick
who never grew up,
               the new
bird from Frinton,
titivating the bay windows
on the foreshore
                with a splash
of eastern promise
and a breath of adventure.

    Well, it was nice
while it lasted.
             Here
at ground level,
grassed off,
it all feels
       a bit
lorn, though.
           I'm high
on half-truth
but she can't fool
me all
      the time,
the tricksy pixy.
          Don't
just go on flying
into the mean distance,
                up
the gennel,
        tell
me if I'm
a liar
    or a lucky

bastard.
         If I rub
my head, I
still hear
         that Irish brogue
and see those green eyes
looking lovesick.
                  So was
it for real
         or
am I (as the others all were)
up Shit Creek
without a compass?

III On Melancholy

It's not a matter
of just forgetting
about it.
         Or wrenching
the caps off
aspirin-bottles.
                  If you're
the awake sort, it
means, baby,
         the beloved
sinking feeling coming
a bit on the slow side, so
                  get wise,
don't start
messing about
         with
quacks and hocus-pocus,
death-watch, butterfly-kisses

of randy evangelists,
                    or
fluff of Tengmalm, it
won't work.

    Whenever you get
the heeby-jeebies, the
                    creeps,
or whatever, like
thunder coming
                when you're out
without an umbrella,
clapping the hoods over
                    the wet leaves
in the whole garden,
                    grave clothes
on your pet mountain,
                    the drill is
to work out on a Sarah Churchill,
or have a run
                by the seaside,
sit in with
packed vases.
                    If it's
your lady-love
giving you gyp,
                    the form is
get a hold of her
by the maulers, and
                    while
she has it off,
give her a tense glare
                    in
the pupils.

228

Remember, she's
the pretty one, it
can't last.

        So turn
over in your mind
the gay wave you got
the last time,

             and the nip
of orgasm, sour
even while they're

                sucking off.
Yes, it's in
the whore-house,

           there
in the back-parlour,
surrounded by the burst

             sachets,
the mysterious
feather boas, and

          the call sign,
splitting the
rhinoceros-pellets

          between your teeth,
that's when
you get the final vision,
gasping your way

          through
to where she straddles

            in spent splendour
the chambers of impotence.

                You're not
more than a fresh girl
in a cool church,
                        now are
you?
                Cross of a few
thousand centuries, and
not much noise,
                        you
got your bland touch
with the country stuff
                        (I grant
you, lusher than mine)
through lasting
                simply,
frocked with tree myths
in ghost-fashion,
                        gods
and us,
                and a garnish
of coy girls, lechers,
rape, riot, and
                        the final
big O.

        It's always
easier on the ear
not to have the
                        music
actually *playing*.
                        I
mean, if the oboe
tickles the fine roots

                    230

of the metaphysical
                        man, not
the material one, you
draw a bonus.
                    As,
for example, that
fine boy there
                        in the clearing, he
won't ever get
what he's after, or
                        see
(for that matter) the
leaves fall,
                    but she'll
be as Camay-fresh
and desirable
                    tomorrow, that
cool bint with
the Jimi Hendrix.

    Once you have
the consummation, it's
your swollen eyes, your
                            morning
sickness and your Alka-
Seltzer.
            Whereas here,
I grant you, they're
all swinging, even
the vocalist,
                and
the trees.
            As for
those kids, warm

in each other's
                    expectations,
aren't they just
having a ball,
                    static
in glazed love,
and with all the new tunes!

    Take the religious
piece, too.
                I agree
it's far better
from the cow's point
                    of view,
not to be having
that funny boy with
                    the dog collar
really getting down
to his carve-up
                    in the grove.
So she goes on
all smooth and flowery, and
                        mooing, too.
Then there's the bare city
beside the water,
                    with the lynch-mob
all gone off to
their blood-letting,
                    and not a soul
left with a bad story
to tell the sheriff
                    about
where they are, and who with.
It helps, it
            helps.

Yes, you have
us all voting
for Miss Timeless,
                    the Greek
bird with the
curvy look.
                She
has it all made,
the cold-as-marble look,
                        the few
twigs in her hair,
the downtrodden stance.
                        When we're
all grey, and fucked up,
(and it's coming)
                    you'll be there,
still charming, a mite cool
maybe, to our minds
                    in our troubles
but (and here's good news)
bearing the same message:
                        life's a bowl
of cherries, if you believe it,
if you believe it, life's
                        a bowl of cherries. That's
the big secret, man,
the only secret.

An Ode to English Food

O English Food! How I adore looking forward to you,
Scotch trifle at the North British Hotel, Princes Street,
Edinburgh. Yes, it is good, very good, the best in Scotland.

Once I ate a large helping at your sister establishment,
the Carlton Hotel on Waverley Bridge overlooking the cem-
etery on Carlton Hill. It was rich, very rich and pleasant. O,
duck, though,

roast, succulent duck of the Barque and Bite, served
with orange sauce, mouth-meltingly delicious! You I salute.
Fresh, tender and unbelievable English duck. Such

luscious morsels of you! Heap high the groaning platter
with pink fillets, sucking pig and thick gammon, celestial chef.
Be generous with the crackling. Let your hand slip with the
gravy trough, dispensing plenty. Yes, gravy, I give you your
due, too. O savoury and delightsome gravy, toothsome over

the white soft backs of my English potatoes, fragrant
with steam. Brave King Edwards, rough-backed in your dry
scrubbed excellence, or with butter, salty. Sweet

potatoes! Dear new knobbly ones, beside the oiled sides
of meaty carrots. Yes, carrots. Even you, dumplings,

with indigestible honey, treacle-streaky things. You
tongue-burners. You stodgy darlings. Tumbled out of the
Marks and Spencer's tin or Mr Kipling silver paper wrapper,
warm and ready except in summer. Cold strawberry sauce,
cream and raspberries. O sour gooseberry pie, dissemble
nothing, squeezed essence

234

of good juice. Joy in lieu of jelly at children's
parties, cow-heel that gives the horn a man seeing my twelve-
year-old buttocks oiled in hospital by a nurse assured me, dirty

old bugger. I eat my six chosen slices of bread,
well buttered, remembering you and your successor the tramp
who stole a book for me. Cracked

coffee cup of the lucky day, betokening mother-love,
nostalgic. Fill with Nescafé and milk for me. It is all great,
sick-making allure of old food, sentiment of the belly. I fill
with aniseed's

parboiled scagliola, porphyry of the balls. With, O
with, licorice, thin straws of it in sherbert, sucked up,
nose-bursting explosives of white powders! Yes,

montage of pre-European Turkish delights obtained
under the counter in wartime, or during periods of crisis, and

O the English sickness of it. Food, I adore you.
Pink-faced and randy! Come to me, mutton chops. Whiskers
of raw chicken-bones, wishes

and plastic cups. Unpourable Tizer. Take me before I
salivate. I require your exotic fineness, taste

of the English people, sweep me off my feet into
whiteness, a new experience. With beer. And with blue twists
of salt in the chip packets. Grease of newspaper. Vinegar of
the winter nights holding hands in lanes after *The Way to the
Stars*. It

is all there. Such past and reticence! O such
untranslatable grief and growing pains of the

235

delicate halibut. The heavy cod, solid as gumboots. And the
wet haddock, North Sea lumber of a long Tuesday's lunch.
Fish and sauce. Nibbles and nutshells. Gulps of draught ale,
Guinness or cider made with steaks. English food, you are all
we have. Long may you reign!

The Painter's Model

I was born in Rome from the yolk of eggs
With a bit of mosaic between my legs.

In Byzantium, I was plated and screwed
Until they discovered *The Art of the Nude*.

Van Eyck was an early performer in flesh,
He laid me under a fine gold mesh.

Hieronymus Bosch had a fertile mind,
He blew me with a clarinet, from behind.

Leonardo was a sadistic bleeder,
I couldn't stand swans, so he made me Leda.

Brueghel was a vicious Flemish brute,
I was varnished by him in my birthday suit.

With Lucas Cranach, life was grim,
There were gropes in water, and then a hymn.

Tintoretto took me along a tunnel,
And a brace of disciples felt up my funnel.

Canaletto made me the colour of rum,
When he oiled my vagina it made me come.

Vermeer of Delft was the first voyeur,
I stripped for his mirror, to make quite sure.

With Rubens, it was the Sabine Rapes
On an apparatus like a bunch of grapes.

Anthony Van Dyke gave me VD
On the back of a sinewy horse, with a flea.

As for Boucher, that versatile frog,
He enjoyed me backwards across a log.

David, the bastard, gave me a dose,
And besides that, he was one of those.

Ingres, too, was inclined to be queer,
He tickled my nipples with a Roman spear.

With Delacroix it was chain-mail vests
And discharging his musket across my breasts.

In England, Rossetti soaped my belly
With what he called pre-Raphaelite jelly.

Burne-Jones needed the boots and hair,
His palette seemed blunted when I was bare.

With Auguste Renoir, I shared a punt,
Only things went blurred when he kissed my— —

With Picasso I nearly did my nut,
I was taken to bits by him, in a hut.

As for Braque, with his *nature morte*,
I don't find all that corpse stuff sport.

With Salvador Dali, life was worse,
He had beetles crawling when I got the curse.

I died at last, a kinetic Venus,
And Jim Dine embalmed me in a polythene penis.

Lady Dracula

Lady Dracula
Flies into my mind,
I hear her wings whistle
An' her teeth grind.

> *Lady Dracula*
> *With long black hair,*
> *Lady Dracula*
> *With red fangs bare*

Lady Dracula
Is hungry for blood,
She digs deep in
An' she sucks real good.

> *Lady Dracula*

With long black hair,
Lady Dracula
With red fangs bare

Lady Dracula
Was once alive,
She drinks men's blood
From nine till five.

Lady Dracula
With long black hair,
Lady Dracula
With red fangs bare

When the sun rises,
She goes to bed,
Lady Dracula:
You'll find her dead.

Lady Dracula
With long black hair,
Lady Dracula
With red fangs bare

The Mayerling Dream

At dead of night
In pouring rain
I dress your body
Inside my brain.

Mary Vetsera
Died at Mayerling
Rudolf shot her
Through the head

I am dead, and you are dead

At mid-morning
In fallen snow
The wheels turn
And we travel slow.
It all happened
Long ago.

Mary Vetsera
Died at Mayerling
Rudolf shot her
Through the head

I am dead, and you are dead

The bed stood
Where the altar stands.
Baron Stockau
Crossed her hands.

In a black coach
Upon my knees
I ride with your body
Through bare trees.

Mary Vetsera's
Ring is gold,
Her hair is white
And her hands are cold.

The wheels turn
And the roads wind,
It all happened
In my mind.

Mary Vetsera
Died at Mayerling
Rudolf shot her
Through the head

I am dead, and you are dead

The Auschwitz Rag

I walk on tip-toe
To the Zyklon B,
They're goin' to crucify
Little me.

Up ahead
Stick men in boots,
Crosses over their
Hatchet suits.

The colonel gestures
When I strip.
I spit at him
An' he feels real hip.

Rip them knickers
Off and dance'

I hear you
Can really prance.

Down go my briefs
An' I step out bare
I show my pussy
Like at a fair.

I make that colonel
Stiff as a post,
With his mouth open
Like he seen a ghost.

Jesus-naked
There in the snow,
I see the crema-
torium glow.

Writhe, body,
Against his fly,
I'm gonna kill you
Before I die.

Jerk off, Man,
For the Fatherland,
I'm juicin' your gun
With my other hand.

Some die by gas,
Some die by knives,
I've used up all
Of my nine lives.

Cool cat, cool cat,
I hear you scream.

Here endeth
The Auschwitz dream.

Cranach's Hunts

I

On the first afternoon
they go out of the white city
into the wood.

One with a flat
red hat
has a feathered neck
on his lance.

One with a black hat
is upon a doe
with his sheathed sword.

In the folded
grey sheets of the river
the stags are dying.

Branched heads
waver like waterweeds.

On the bank
seven dogs
beset a hooped one.

Thrown as if
by a tree
one lies in a mat
of its own blood.

In a nearby boat
ladies in long dresses
are rowing.

One is being
groped
by a friar.

The spire of
the church
and the blue peak
assure the world
of a fine day.

After all, the king is hunting.

II

On the second afternoon
they have crossed the
bridge
and are in the firs

with their white swords
erect.

Head down
a stag
is already
under their hooves.

The tongues
of the dogs
flicker
over its body.

In threshed
water
the rest
move their
crowns of thorns.

Today
the ladies
make the shapes of breasts
with their bows.

The church
is nowhere to be seen.

Far off,
the city is roofed in blood.

In a green clearing
all the does in the world
walk naked
before a serving-man
in a grey helmet.

The light
still glistens in their pupils.

The date is 1544.

It might have been yesterday.

Scenes from a History Book

A short man
with a pinched look
and a high moustache
walks fast
up the Judengasse.

They try to sell him
a leather jacket,
a black Homburg hat,
a pair of driving gloves.

He shakes his head,
thrusting his hands
in the pockets of his
belted raincoat.

There is a cold wind.

They laugh,
exchange words
in their fur-lined overcoats.

He hurries on
to the Rathausplatz.

There is a lot to do.

No, he is not Napoleon.
It is 1913.
I give you three guesses who he is.

II

Where did they come from?

They came from
a village in Poland.

These are the cheap tailors
who died in Warsaw.

There are shreds of hair
still on their shoulders,
gold teeth in their pockets.

We never knew, we never knew

It is 1945.

They walk towards
a concrete room
in another city.

I hear the shot.

They laugh,
warming their hands
at the body burning.

Any old hair, any old gold

I smell the petrol
burning flesh
flames rising
black smoke

old clothes
old clothes

Who'll give a penny for Hitler's clothes?

Episode from a Fortnight in Hell

On the thirteenth day
a tiny silver snail
with a sword through its neck
screams on a rock.

Armies quiver and lunge
like porcupines.

Dinosaurs, or perhaps
camels,
mount a hill towards a castle.

On a stone
like a toad, corpses
are grouped,
ready for shovelling into the ravine.

They call this *Understanding Each Other's Point of View*.

Orlando Enters the Common Market

I

What did we win the war for?
    (Orlando thought)
as he passed the PANZER DELICATESSEN

    See them everywhere
nowadays.

        BLOODY WOGS
        NIGGERS
        JEWBOYS

    If I had my way,
I'd flog the ruddy
        lot of them.

        DIRTY BASTARDS

II

    Oh yes, Mr Eisenstadt,
I think the new Eurovision
        car-wash
is a very flash idea.

    Go a bomb, I'd say.

    Why, only yesterday
I was saying to Mrs Orlando
        (wasn't I, bunny)

    why can't we all let
bygones be bygones

and realize it's
1970

and we have to lick the arse
of the fucking German people
        whether we

like it or not,
        don't we now?

This was one of Orlando's
right-wing days.

The Political Orlando

i *Orlando in Chicago*

Last year, Orlando
went to Chicago

                for the famous party conference.

        There he met,
one after another,
        three jolly American policemen.

        The first one
hit him with a night-stick
        across the foreskin.

The second one
spat a wad of half-chewed shag
    all over the blue grass of Illinois.

    The third one
just stood and fingered the butt of his pistol
    like it was some kind of a
surrogate penis.
             After that experience,
Orlando came home,
a sadder but a wiser man.

Next year,
Orlando will go to the moon.

II *Orlando Goes to the Moon*

    In every particular,
we are the imperialists of the Sea of Tranquillity
    according to Orlando,

or will be,
when he gets there.

Three for the sea-saw:
    the Plain of Jars
    the Bay of Pigs
    and the Sea of Tranquillity

Orlando knows them all,
their qualities,
        and how to put quite a good face
on why the Stars and Stripes
had to be pinned there.

251

Quite a story,
how Orlando got his Purple Heart.

III *Orlando in Vietnam*

Now it can be told:

Orlando is on
a search and destroy mission.

Over the roof-tops
he goes with his claws out
in a chopper.

From a small 7-transistor radio set
he will keep in earshot
of the top thirty.

Some of them, a select few,
may even be in there with him,
wide-eyed
and bushy-tailed.

Orlando is facing out
the VCs
eyeball to eyeball.

If he isn't careful,
Orlando is going to win
another medal.

Orlando will have a
ticker-tape welcome
back in Yawnsville, Massachusetts,

where the worst that ever happens
is the local dentist
        having his wisdom teeth out.

        Ah me, thought Orlando
(reading this)
        if only a few others,
            naming no names,
had had their wisdom teeth put in!

Orlando is quite a philosopher.

The Jules Verne Orlando

I

Orlando is thinking:

I shall go a journey
        to the centre of Orlando,
and see what's going on there.

II

Pretty dark in here.

        Strike a light, someone.

SHIVERING STILTS!

What a lot of nasty creepy-crawlies.

253

III

      You are now entering
the famous ORANGE room.

      Here, the ORANGE poet
wrote the original
      perfect
      (and now famous)

      ORANGE POEM.

Orlando gazes in awe.

GOSH, IT'S FUN

      Later,
he meets the giant lizards.

Orlando's Love Life

I

      The scene
is a bent attic bedroom
      somewhere in Hampstead.

      Overhead
the German bombers
      drone home,

I LOVE YOU, I LOVE YOU
  screams Orlando.

  Well, wouldn't you,
with a 27-year-old
  undischarged schizophrenic
holding a bread knife
  over your balls?

II

KNOCK KNOCK
KNOCK KNOCK

  Who's there?

Colonel Orlando
  has come, Madam.

  Well, I haven't,
so tell him to keep on knocking.

  (aside) The insolence
of these military people!

III

  Orlando, though,
had a high opinion
  of the love relationship.

  He knew quite a few
of the best people in the business
  for fornicating.

255

Oh yes,
Orlando loves them all,
the red, the white and the khaki.

Only one little lady
with a mouth the size of *The Aspern Papers*
has his heart in her honeysuckle, though.

The Orange Poem

Not very long ago
One morning
I sat in my orange room
With my orange pencil
Eating an orange.

This,
I began to write,
Is the orange poem.
I shall become known
As the orange poet

For inventing
And first writing
The original
Perfect
And now famous

ORANGE POEM
Which this is.

Having written which
In my orange room
With my orange pencil

I turned over a new leaf
Which this is.
Meanwhile,
Inside the orange poem
A small man

Wth an orange pencil
Sat in an orange room
Eating an orange.
This, he began to write,
Is the orange poem.

A Spell to Make a Hedgehog Return

hérisson, hérisson

Word for a pig, word for a sow,
word for an ugly old woman,

word for the point of a spear,
word for a thorn,
word for a harrow,

ireçon, ireçon

hiding in sheaves of corn,
      in bales of hay,
hiding in rushes cut for thatching,

pitched into a wagon,
      crossing the sea on faggots to Amrun,
stranded on floating logs,
      on floating islands of turf,

Algerian,
      with a bald patch,
long-eared,
      between the Caspian and the Sea of Azov,
with a narrow skull in the steppe and the desert,
      or in the gorges of the Balkans,

      riccio, riccio

      Word for a pig, word for a sow,
      word for an ugly old woman,

      word for the point of a spear,
      word for a thorn,
      word for a harrow,

      ireçon, ireçon

feeding on worms,
      on wood-lice,
feeding on apples and fungi,
      on eggs of the corn-crake,

living in small caves,
      in the burrows of shelldrakes,
living in cracks in the rocks,

in hollow tree-trunks,
living in walls of dry stone,
in the under-floor spaces of barns,
living in arched roots,
in tangled old heather,
in thatched reeds,

erizo, erizo

Word for a pig, word for a sow,
Word for an ugly old woman,

word for the point of a spear,
word for a thorn,
word for a harrow,

ireçon, ireçon

hérisson,
ireçon,
riccio,
erizo, veni,

in nomine erinacei primi, veni

Homage to Arcimboldo

i The Lesser Horned Artichoke

This rare and

captured
one squats
in a sieve,

hissing. It
marshals
its host
of peaked leaves, wanting

to bring
something to birth. It
hatches a
plan, spits

froth of
a buttery
stew
in

a pan. It
makes its name,
dies,
and is eaten, leaf by leaf, to the bone.

ii The Male Sea Asparagus

In its
eternal
search
for a mate, the

male
sea asparagus
advances
with all its appendages. It

finds
its glaucous
love
subdued

in a heart-white
napkin,
nude
before

the ravages
of the sea. It
enters
her sighing.

iii *The Spider-Hunting Aubergine*

After dark,
with the shepherd's-crook
of its antennae
out, this gloomy predator

stalks through
the dusky glades.
There,
knitting its orbs,

all unawares,
the great leviathan
of the silk works
is lurking.

One touch
of those poisonous
mandibles
and that furry arachnid

261

is a goner.
Then
that gross aubergine
lays its eggs in her belly.

iv *The Masked Avocado*

It is
a poor ball
or function that is not graced
by the masked

avocado,
cane,
skin, and *vinaigrette*.
Through both

of its black eyes
this gay seducer
cons
the midnight world

of the sea-bed
or the dance-floor.
Extending
a bark-like claw

from the sands of time,
it sucks,
most elegantly,
a little dry, enclosed air in.

v The Short-Toed Runner Bean

In its green
winkle-pickers, this
inconspicuous
creature

fades
without a
sound
into the dusk. At

midnight
when the elves
are
foraging, and

trees creep
into
their own
shadows, you

sometimes see
one
eviscerating
a pair of transfixed nail-clippers.

vi The Crab-Eating Beetroot

With its raw
maw, and
vertiginous
appetite

for lung-worms, you
would scarcely

credit how
many

small crustacean items
it can
pack away, this
haunter

of the ice-floes,
immaculate
as a red whale.
All things

with claws avoid it.
In a good season,
we sometimes
harpoon one with a scythe.

vii The False Cabbage

There is only
one
way to prove
the false cabbage.

Place
your reluctant visitor
on the back
of a clean envelope,

extract
one ounce
of green blood
from

its tail
or hindquarters, and
suck
the offending substance

into your
nostrils.
If it be false,
a noxious fume will swell forth.

viii The North American Whooping Carrot

It sounds
off at the most unexpected
moments. Just
when you think it might be time

for lunch, it
sweats out
its protest. Far away
in the mountains of somewhere

like Utah, you
hear it whooping it up
with the Swedes,
very loudly.

I dare say
it *is* rare, but
I don't hold
with all that:

oink oink
it says, though,
like a man with a bad cough,
repeating himself.

ix *The True Cauliflower*

Others
may seem to be
it, but the
true

variety wears
its heart
on its sleeve.
Leafing

through an old
bed
of bean-shoots,
or a cabbage-plot,

you might
come on one,
white
and a little shaken,

with its
ear
to the ground,
hearing no evil.

x *The Little Brown Celery*

As it wanders
through
the grisly forests
of the kitchen-garden,

the little brown
celery

is accustomed
to sing:

Three bare
patches in
the cabbage-bed.
Three bare

caterpillars
learning to
fly.
Cabbage-white,

cabbage-white,
soar in the sky.
I shall be a salad
before I die.

xi *The Great Crested Cucumber*

It runs
to a chill,
baize
crescent, as

sharp
as
a claymore in
the dry flesh

of sandwiches. It
evicts
dead
butter, bread

267

rolls, dodging
the webbed
fingers
of the vicar's wife

at garden-parties. It
roams,
unsliceably deranged,
through the bean-rows.

xii The Pigmy Sperm Leek

If you cut
one open, it
screams,
yielding

a black pus
before
knife or
vagina. Vicious

in captive
solitude, it
yanks
its hair out

of the ground,
bewailed
by the Israelites.
Tainting

the breath, it
remembers
the crime of Onan, spilling
its own seed.

xiii The Slow Lettuce

It goes
on one hinged leaf
over the soil,
shoe-horning itself

into
whatever
plots it
finds vacant. It

spends
a dry
week on its bed,
sluggishly. It

evaluates the
perforated
spaces of its
own abdomen

as if
about to begin
a most catholic sentence. Its
last word is *prey*.

xiv The Vampire Marrow

If ever
you walk
after dark
in

the quieter parts
of

your own
intestines, watch

out
for the inky, tar-like
excrement
of the vampire

marrow. It
snores
all day
in a hole, stretching

only
at midnight,
with its wings beating,
for a bite to eat.

xv The Hammer-Headed Mushroom

It swims
in its own
oil,
arcs

along the rock
shelves
of the hind mind. It
spouts

a voluminous
white water,
dying
into the

failed light
of
an Arctic
solitude. It

spins
its melon slice of
a mouth, inhaling
a scent of leaves.

xvi The Death-Watch Onion

As if at a wake,
it weeps
in the ceiling, wears
mourning hues

in its layered
hair, as
its bleak young
hatch and

fly. Be
not fooled by
such
behaviour. Its

black
jaws are already
at work
in your drawers. That

cracking
that you hear

271

is
their broken hearts.

xvii *The Hooded Parsnip*

It stoops
through
the wet forests
of Ayrshire, as

white and
vulnerable
as an old woman. At
the witching hour

it snouts
earth
up
from the bottom

of a stiff
mound, rumpling
its
ashen hair as

it aches
into
a sitting position
near to the moon.

xviii *The Bottle-Nosed Pea*

It flaunts
a bulge
in its forehead, owns
intelligence

like
a cyst of corrupt water. It
rolls,
boiled,

through the glass
waves
of jars, bruising
its nose. Emitting.

a
glutinous
and oily
wax, it

becomes
hated, hunted. Then
it explodes,
blubbering, in a scalding lash of fluked light.

xix The Solitary Pepper

It goes
alone over the
blasted heath,
sneezing. Its

rugged
face confronts
ill winds that
bode

nobody good, as
it licks
dandelions
bare

of pollen, wanders
into
the purlieus
of the sallow

catkins, asks
only
for a little bit of bread
and no cheese.

xx *The Pyrenean Mountain Potato*

All winter,
sick
on the dry
smell of brandy, it

soils
its own furrow
with
a hot manure. But

when
the sun explodes
from dust
in

the fresh summer, it
splays
broad feet
over

new ground,
horny,

white-furred, and
sweet as iron on the tongue.

xxi The Hollow-Faced Radish

It moans
like a lantern
swinging
in fog, roots

through old
rubbish dumps
for a bone. When
it hears

the cramp of dustbins
closing, it
screws
those leathery filaments

in
its ears to
their blank crunch,
scavenging.

It grows
on the backs of
mole-skulls,
depositing vermin.

xxii The Cream Long-Hair Tomato

For all
the
rotundity
of its thick

sides, this
light herb
assails
heights of the glass-house

with
a pursed lip. It
climbs with
a sort of swollen,

glacial
disdain, running
to
seed. It sheds light, hiding

in the graceful
veils
of a beady-eyed
frogs'-spawn.

xxiii The Giant Woolly Turnip

All year
it lurks
in the turf,
thick

as a bomb. But
at Hallowe'en,
uprooted,
randy,

it gropes out
by lantern-light
of its own
bowels,

yowling
for food. With
a sweating
mob

of hot Swedes, it
stumbles
into a bonfire, crackling,
and is burnt alive.

xxiv The Pale Clouded Yellow Water-cress

It
breaks
from a chrysalis
of lips, is

a film
of
gauze on
the black

sponge
disintegrating
in shell holes. It
breathes a scent of mustard. In

all
the seven hours it
flies
before

salting
its grave

in the bean-row, it
never winces, lies, or empties its lungs of blood.

Lamps

I

  as if
burning
  seeds of

a pomegranate
  in
cabriole ivory, you

  exude
thunderstorms of
  immaculate plastic

II

  lascivious
root, emerging
  fatigued

  through
tight, lacy
  knickers of

  seven
iridescent
  nipples

III

    dragon's
pierced orifice
     on

a bracket,
    hinged
for a massacre

    amidst
degenerate
    toadstools

IV

    reflections of
tulips, blur
    through smoke,

    as if
'designed for a Cleveland man'
    meant

    only fluting, a
crinkle edge
    to cigars

V

    Russian
lemons, dipped
    from

    a fluorescent
balloon of
    wasp-waisted

elastic, as
delicate as a monkey's
   testicles

VI

   metallic
wedding cake, a
   ticklish

   howdah
submerging
   a single

   enormous
acorn's
   incandescence

VII

   as a spider
clawing
   over a ceiling

   hooked
with obstreperous
   tiles,

   bloat,
raw, and uneasy,
   you steal

The Sirens

I grope for time
In its precise cold place.
   Violence is bright
Behind my hollow eyes
That milk the war for rhyme.
   That sound is lies
I say began each night

And was the one
Remembered by the few
   Tied to the mast
Who lived. I hear it grate
Against the April sun,
   Then separate
As fragments, and blow past.

The War

I seem to hear,
In those bombed houses where
   I echoed in
The empty rooms,
      An air

As if, in their
Consumed expanses, what
   Was there before

This living chill
    Is not

A smell of rot
Only, and mouldered wood,
    But something more
    Like an old skin
        That could,

If someone would
Renew its odour, smack
    Of warmth, and life,
    And what consumes,
        For lack

Of fuel, crack
As timber, or as mines,
    Hushed, like that one
    Whose early fall
        Refines

All that my lines
Here and before contain,
    And makes them burn
    Into a grief
        Again.

The Passing Ones

They do not die.
Moved to another shelf,
They lie in shadow. Where
The bombers fly

To burn Cologne,
Rain drenches the cold air.
I wake, and ask myself,
Hearing their drone

And echo, where
My father is, whose death
Was thirty years ago.
I halt them there,

Beating the sky
Into the mould of bread.
Their pilots live. Their breath
Injures me. Why

Do those I know
Retire into blank snow
And freeze there, as if dead?
The minutes flow

Into a bowl
Where people scald, and flare
Like tapers. In my bed
I sense the whole

Burial of parts,
Rib, liver, guts and brain.

I know the worm, the crow
    Gagging at hearts,

    At lights, at ends
Of all we were, and are.
I threaten what has fled.
    I call my friends

    Out of the soil
And from the funeral jar
To come in blood again,
    I hear, in oil

    And petrol, one
Remembered scrap-iron car
Start where its owner bled
    And someone gun

    The two-stroke, sure
Of where he has to head,
North to the border. Far
    Behind him, pure

    As cream, or snow,
A woman with a hat
Settles to grief and pain.
    All that, I know,

    I may say here
In Germany, on a train,
Writing through dark like tar,
    Must seem from fear

    That I shall lie
As they both do in earth.

I say what I have said:
    They do not die.

    Turning, they try
To hide from other birth
And be, as when first wed,
    Withdrawn to a high

    Moment, on shelves
Above the meat of things,
Where they can dream, and wait,
    And be themselves.

The Dying Calf

    So rising late
That Saturday, we drove towards the sea,
Tired from our show. And having parked the car,
Walked in a dream of caring, past the slate
And shale of Westbay. There, below the cliff,

    Half-caked with mud,
A calf had fallen. Shivering, it lay
Like broken driftwood, near the tideline. If
The air had feathers for the cold, some should
Have settled there. On stones of unconcern

    The seaborn light
Watered a space wherein the body spread
Its final claim, to make our footsteps turn

And be Samaritan. As others might,
If they believed, we thought that it would live,

     And so walked back,
And telephoned a vet, and waited there,
Four caring ones. One talked. One tried to give
Some thought to verse. One laid his anorak
Along its back. I watched the muddy hide

     As it pulsed, pulsed. So
When the police came, and carried it away
Still living, in a sack, I felt no pride
Or stupid hope. Its death seemed long ago,
Stripping all muscle from the bones of verse

     And making love
Like we had shown dishonest. Pausing, as
The sun came out of clouds, I felt the curse,
Placed like a falcon on our brows, above
And near the eyes, the curse of caring, pass

     And stoop to ground
Along the sand. Across the sea, far out
I saw the light fall, turning, with no sound
Over and over, as we talked about
Our poetry, and die along the grass.

Poem before Birth

Rising from bed
I shaved. Outside, the birds awoke
And sang in pleasure through the rising mist
With bells and cars. Then something turned and spoke
    Inside my borrowed head
These words that follow, and were found. Light kissed

The ploughland, white
With naked scythes. If it was Love,
Or what I wanted to believe was that,
I hardly knew then. But in air, above
    The sparrow's broken flight,
Returning from his nightlong hunt, the cat

Saw the fine day
And mewed for joy. I heard, and shared
His bleat of praise. As others rose, and made
The old wood flustered, as if it, too, cared
    Throughout your house, I say
I never knew how far Love was obeyed.

The clock's low snore
Resounded in its brazen frame
To help the time. The wind made fastened leaves
Turn in the larches. And the cherished flame
    That fell in ash before
The gathering of darkness, clasped in sheaves

Like wheat. The chair
I sat in seemed to flower, and snow
To roses with a scent. Inside my throat
The wine of our good meal began to slow

And wake to vineyards. Bare
In my new body's fort, I touched the moat

    Round my content
  And felt in love. So I wrote out
At peace, and for my pleasure, these few words
To thank my evening host. Here, never doubt,
    I have to say, in scent
Of burning pine, to touch the air with birds,

    Joy comes. Today
  So honoured by the care of friends
I rise to feel safe. And when time begins
And nothing but the emptying cellar ends
    With breakfast, and the way
Towards another room, life moves on fins

    In water, child
  Swimming to birth. So I, who praise
My lodging in a doctor's house, approve
Ceremonies of beneficence. That blaze
    Along your windows, wild
As what went hunting all night long, was Love.

The Broken Ones

    Today I hear
Through troubled iron of my own concerns
Of how his are. He speaks, as always, in

That strangled candour, and my whole world burns
As he announces marriage. I begin.

　　　　Through violent air
To dwindle from his days. Outside, black rain
Slants across London. An Alsatian runs
To and fro past his penthouse. And again
I crush my papers, wishing they were guns

　　　　And we at war
With someone. Years away, in Furness Fields,
I see boys running, buttered by the mud,
At war with Westbourne. One boy scores, one yields
A face of stiffened longing. Where we stood

　　　　At school, in time,
The years are melting. Others are in tune
Along the naked wires. The broken places
Focus and die. A boy is beaten. Soon
Stripes in the cheeks will fade, the burning traces

　　　　Alter and fail.
I mount the rostrum, anguished in my grace
To read the lesson, furnish them with souls.
Power never known. All falter in the race,
Thrashed down like fish. Set breathless into bowls,

　　　　Glassed from our world,
The great sea rising, we become that sperm
I feel one summon, prick out, in a shed.
The death's-head lifts another like a worm
Outside the Gardens, and that power is dead

　　　　Wherein we lived
In fettered honour. On this telephone

I live again my childhood, the soaked head
Raging against maturity, the bone
White from my father's body, never shed

    Save as long tears
Gliding along the window. Whirled, and lost,
The past goes tortured into earth, and spoils,
Foundering, and useless. On my skin, embossed,
I bear the medals of those burning oils

    Torn from a shell
And severing his future. By the wall
There in the kitchen, still delivered, she
I stride and open in all women, tall
And flat before death's onslaught, mothers me

    With love I hate,
Spit back, and spurn. So in this office, dressed
In cured skin from a world I want to share,
I watch a dog run barking, held and blessed
By his master's caring. And I turn to prayer,

    Not for myself,
Though that has been, but for my closest friend,
The polio-torn, the brave one. Cracked and spewed
From the world's belly, that will never mend,
I ask the blood-shot to let up their feud

    For a short space
And honour him, as I. May he and his
Through casts of measured silence and true sound
Flourish and never sicken. May his alliance
Bleed into glory from far underground

And rise in sons
To blaze for ever in the night of shells
That bred us in the North. May he in joy
Walk through the morning to the chant of bells
And wake in marriage. May no power destroy

That healing love
I see, and fall from. Turning to the flame
That seems to burn for ever in my head,
I settle from his changing, still the same,
Loving the broken ones, the never dead.

On the Death of May Street

for my grandfather

You built it, and baptized it with her name,
Sixty-eight years ago. No angel came

That first Edwardian day to plant the stone
And make a child. Your wife conceived alone

And bore my mother in that soaking room
Where water later flowed, that choked her womb.

Tonight I write that May Street is condemned
And sure to die, as she was. Gripped and hemmed

By the sour blood of change, that rips and kills,
It dies far quicker than she did by pills.

I own it, and I see it broken, stone
By mother-naked stone. I heard her groan

That last night in our house before she died,
Not knowing how to help her. So I cried,

As I do now inside, to see her name
Shaken, and wasted. For your wasted fame

I cry to you, grandfather, in your grave
In rage and grief. All that you failed to save

Has shrunk to geometry, to crumbled lime
Beside the brickworks, to your grandson's rhyme.

Sarah's Room

Proust got rushes when his rats were
Punctured with a pin

The door is clinking on the latch,
   And no one now is in:
The kitchen stirs. And Sarah's room
   Shivers like my sin.

Sarah is out, and I am here,
   Alone upon her mat.
I lie and write a loving note,
   With drawings of a cat.

The logs are sinking on her hearth,
  It's growing rather late.
The pictures that I gave her burn
  Against the blackened slate.

I remember, I remember,
  A dog that ran away.
Sarah's head was in my hand,
  And Rover's hair was grey.

Stop the picture, close the flies,
  I can hear a car.
The Wonder Book of Reptiles wants me,
  And the door's ajar.

I mean I knew, I mean I knew,
  It was quite a thing
Polishing a bit of rubber
  To make a wedding ring.

The door is clinking on the latch,
  And someone else is in.
I am in the garden, and
  Sarah's in the bin.

    Proust got rushes when his rats were
    Punctured with a pin

Lovers

One night we ate, and then lay down
  Under a slab of stone.
The Green was dark, and dog-shit stank
  Against my ankle-bone.

That happened later. At the time
  I noticed only fox,
Smell of her coat along the ground,
  And pressure of a box.

The wind was cold. We lay and screwed,
  As happy as we could.
I mean, you're better off out there
  Than wormed-through under wood.

So we got home. Unsatisfied,
  She lay and watched the stars.
Far off, a hundred yards away,
  I heard the passing cars.

We cleaned my shoe with soap. It stank
  For days on end of shit.
So did her kitchen. As she said,
  You're never shot of it.

It's true. Last night, I dreamed of her,
  Jealous, and vaguely lost.
I woke, and took a parcel in,
  And wondered what it cost.

The sense of death, the sense of loss,
  A sort of worried guilt.

Yes, it was worth it, as we were,
    Better than with a quilt

Hours later. So we had it off
    Amidst the corpses there.
Her skirt was up above her thighs,
    Four inches of them bare.

That, and the dog-shit, I recall,
    And will in later years.
Broken lady, flaunt your columns,
    Virginity is tears.

Gloria's Letter

I

Dear John, I thought you'd like to know,
    I'll kill you, if I can,
Unless you leave your childish wife,
    And learn to be a man.

It's getting more than I can bear
    To live alone up here
In Hampstead, and I want you back,
    As soon as may be, dear.

II

Well, well, I thought, that's rather bad,
    I'd better lock the door.
But still, she'll come and scream outside,
    And call my wife a whore.

The telephone's still on the hook,
    And soon we'll hear it ring.
A woman scorned feels pretty tough,
    And Gloria's mind's like string.

It ties you up in cutting knots
    Until your sinews burn.
You can't get loose however much
    You try to twist and turn.

So drive to her, says I to me,
    As naked as a pear.
It won't do any good, you know,
    To kiss her lovely hair.

So take her nipples in your hands
    With all the skill you've got,
And that, from what the papers say,
    Is really quite a lot.

III

Dear John, it wouldn't do, my boy,
    I'm not so daft as that.
I've bought some liquor for my friend,
    And locked us in my flat.

If you come there, the police will come,
    And throw you into jail,

Frustrated as a leper with
  A can tied to your tail.

So go away, or come away,
  Be mine, or never mine,
You bloody, stupid, little, fucking,
  Meretricious swine!

Time Passing

I

And did they run
Together down
Towards the sea? And was it dark?
And who was there?

Was anyone
Besides the two
Sisters? Was Aubrey there? And was
It really cold?

II

And was the tide
Receding, with
An undertow? And did they care?
And did the girls

Change on the sands,
Or beforehand

In the caravan? And did the moon
Come out and show

Them shivering
Between the groynes,
Their bodies whetted, rubbed with salt,
And bare as knives

Mounting the water as
The kings and queens
On playing cards? And did they laugh
And fall in waves?

III

And did their hands
Or icy hips
Touch underwater, and withdraw?
And did the surge

Pull down their hearts
To its own cold?
And did the night
Seem long and full

With empty riches,
And the world
Float in their eyes
For a great distance?

IV

Yes. It did.
And did the watch
One dropped as he
Came wading in

Jam, with the time
For ever in
Its glassy face? And is it there
Imperishable in

The green, a joy
And care to come
For all of them? And will they know
Before they die?

v

No. They will not.
And as they dry
Their sanded flesh
And walk away, a bitter wind

Whitens the breath
Each gives to air.
And do they know?
No. They do not. And never will.

1 September 1972

The World of J. Edgar Hoover

There wasn't time to take a gun, and follow through the turns.
Nothing to do but hammer back, with a halo and your burns.

I go into Chicago, and I go into Yale,
And they take my face with a proper grace, and a plate of rice
and kale.

299

Somebody was clever, and somebody was true,
Their hats were down on their hard eyes, and they died to
make me glue.

Talk to Alexander, and talk to Hitler, too,
They weren't the same as I was, with their heads and their men
in blue.

If anything could matter, it wasn't where you were
The night they caught Capone, and tossed him in the stir.

Black eyes, blue eyes, it's all the same in hell
When they ring the bloody changes, and you crack the passing
bell.

I took out my revolver, and I took it out to kill,
With a death's-head on my harness, and a tranquillizing pill.

I cried for my machine gun, I cried to make them come,
The women with the honey, and the men who turned their
thumb.

So try a little harder, and keep your money shut,
The world slows to stardom, and all police-work's for a slut.

America, I loved you, I hung you on my wall,
As anxious and exotic as a show-girl at a ball.

Now it's nearly over, I lie and scream in bed
For a handful of your hard nuts, and some silence in my head.

I hear the fires frying, and the cannon in my brain,

And the past seems to gush and spurt like rubbish down a
drain.

'Listen, Mr Hoover, I need a place to go' –
OK, so make it Sing-Sing, and take your ten years slow.

I broke him for his arrogance, he took a money rap,
And another with his brother, like a ferret in a trap.

I get explicit dying, I can hear the choppers clack,
Or are they red-neck ravens, with a warrant on their back?

Into ice and shadow, into night I come,
With an ice chip on my shoulder, and a last glass of rum.

'Listen, Mr Hoover, it's 1972,
And the skids are on the century, and all you tried to do.

So it's out with Al Capone, and it's out with Dillinger,
And as for Mistress Bonny, why, you've had your lot of her.'

Well, let them scream and settle, the vultures on my time,
I never heard of any state that never heard of crime.

I took it by its rough throat, I shook it into life,
And for fifty years it came to bed, and I screwed it like a wife.

So lie and love your little men, your Johnsons and your Jews,
I'm not afraid of how it sounds when you read it in the news.

I was the man who pushed them, I held their sweating hands,
And I cleaned their bottoms for them, at the hokey-pokey
stands.

'Into Guatemala now, or anywhere at all,
Into Cuba, into Vietnam,' hear the bugles call

Just like Kipling for the limeys, beautiful and clear:
All they saw was theirs to have, and they broke it like a steer.

'Yes, but we had our reasons, we had to do what's right' –
And I was there to clear the mess, and sweep the shit from
sight.

I was the cause and action, I watched with a cold eye
Their life and death, as Yeats did, like a cadillac pass by.

Heaped with flowers, and letters, your century goes down, ·
As masterful as Nineveh, and as cruel as a clown.

The wheels are turning slowly, and the mafia slope arms,
Before your Irish wolf-hounds, with their red hair and their
charms.

The hearse is made of walnut, and the mounts are brass and
gold,
And underneath the lot I lie, like an egg kept warm in mould,

The conscience of your blood-lust, and the broomstick of your
will,
As useless to the future as a government by skill.

Tomorrow to Belfast I ride, and tomorrow to Japan,
With a Thomson gun, or an atom bomb, and a throw of sand
in a pan.

It never ends, the violence. It drives, and always will.
So take your time, and think it out, and remember who must
kill.

The professionals, like I was, know. We take it in our stride,
And what we can't dispose of quick, we learn the way to hide.

Good night, America. And drop me in the ground.
Let the earth fall across my chest, like the muzzle of a hound.

Elegy for the Gas Dowsers

When you douse for gas, you
put your finger in a pipe:
the flesh must be warm,
and the water ripe,
the guts in the ground
the texture of tripe

I

I see the bare vowels
        funnelling for space:
men trying
        to push them into place.
Out at sea,
        they can hear the tide race.

Here, it's a business
        of sewage and piles:
blocked tubes
        for miles on miles.
The water flares,
        and you've lost your files.

I don't see much hope
 for a change of scene,
with some high kicking
 in the Park, or the Green.
It's the North Sea,
 or the dream-machine.

II

With the bowels tunnelled
 by so much slime,
you have to be at it
 all the time:
shit-shooting
 with a ball of rime.

In winter, sheepskin,
 in summer, goat's:
the men running
 for bedraggled coats.
I don't believe you've seen
 so many floats.

The ball cock's rising,
 the plunger drops:
and, out by the lighthouse,
 a razor chops.
Spume flying,
 poisoned crops.

III

Anywhere, cleansing:
 business for grabs.
The boys in their zips
 when the cancer jabs.

And then, heaving
    corpses on slabs,

all terror
    all hate,
and the ugly look
    of the foetus, in a grate.
A broken window,
    then glue on a plate.

If it seizes up,
    you can go and see:
dripping tunnels
    and the smell of pee;
like a jellyfish
    by the side of the sea.

IV

Who else would do it?
    When there's only rust,
and the scuffle of rat's feet,
    stale crust,
soiled knickers
    and tissues thrust

in the blown gaps.
    There have to be holes,
and we have to fill them
    with blood, and poles.
It doesn't matter if
    the ship rolls.

Tight-holding,
    belly-firm,

the dousers are anchored
in their own sperm:
others' organs
convulse like worm.

v

They go with nausea,
filthy, old:
their eyes watering,
feet in mould.
These are men with
their bodies sold.

They police whatever
stinks and rots:
where the blue smell
of a gas escape blots.
Pretty city!
Underneath, it knots.

In the wind, in sewers,
over the heath,
a stench drifts
as you draw breath:
the final, exhausted
smell of death.

When you douse for gas, you
put your finger in a pipe:
the flesh must be warm,
and the water ripe,
the guts in the ground
the texture of tripe

306

A Kipling Situation

The water churned to fragments
    Out in Algeciras Bay,
With the yellow tugs escorting
    A destroyer on her way

Past the tanker, stretched at anchor
    In the foreground, by the mole,
With her lights already winking
    As her decks begin to roll,

Spain far off to starboard,
    Africa to port,
And the stiff flag flying
    On the Old Moorish fort,

It's a Kipling situation,
    And it needs a Kipling beat,
As I sit and watch the night fall
    With black marble at my feet.

II

Nelson won his victory
    Where the spume is on the sea,
And the dry dock's rusting,
    And the women drink their tea

In the Rock Hotel. At sundown,
    The pool is icy cold,
And the wind is in the palm tree,
    And the pine is very old,

And the dream is losing colour
    As the water loses light,
Where the pale destroyer shrivels
    Into nothing. Out of sight,

Out of earshot, out of smell,
    Out of taste, and mind,
Nothing left but salt and echoes,
    Smoke left black behind

On the white air, drifting slowly
    Towards a darkening shore,
It's a Kipling situation, and
    I don't want it any more.

Gibraltar, 1972

The Cretins

O heavens! is't possible a young maid's wits
Should be as mortal as an old man's life?

Hamlet, Act IV, Scene v

I

There was something about that night,
    and the restaurant, and the food:
we thought about Proust, and his book,
    and both remembered the past

as we ate our bread and cheese,
    and watched the flow of the sea
where it seemed to move like a river
    away towards the west.

I thought about Normandy,
    and the beaches that other June
nearly thirty years before,
    and the storm the night they came.

And then it happened: the moment
    changed, and defined for ever
by a tiny incident
    so rich it burned like a sore.

II

They were brought along the shore
    led by a group of nuns,
all dressed in their plain blue scarves:
    and they stopped for the setting sun.

They stood with their arms held wide,
    and their heavy faces fixed
on the simple glow in the air:
    and some of them sang a hymn.

It was piteous, it was grim.
  I felt the long tears wax
in my eyes as the red ball fell
    into the sea, and died.

From the window, I could see
    the pleasure it gave their minds
blocked from the cradle, to feel
    the last heat of the day

and to take its joy on their skin
    and to hold it gently there,
more full of its dwindling fire
    than anyone else could be.

Cabourg, June 1973

Death of a Ferrari

In Memoriam 840 HYK

I

It was made for the manager of Crockford's,
    Driven in a Monte Carlo Rally,
Owned by a salesman, later, at Maranello's,
    A retired colonel, then me.

I couldn't afford that wastrel elegance.
    I could scarcely carry
The seven-foot, iron exhaust system
    When it cracked, and broke, in Leeds.

I loved its worn, greyed ivory leather,
    The petrol-blue of its hide.
It growled along at 104
    With its bad brakes, and its leaking seal.

I can hear now that famous,
    Belly-flustering Ferrari roar

Bounced back off the wall of the underpass
    One night, in Piccadilly. It was like the Blitz.

All right. So the door was rusted,
    Smoke came out of the dashboard wires
The first time I drove it on the M4.
    Who cares? It was a major car.

II

It didn't crash on the motorway,
    Or blow up at 150.
It didn't burn itself out down a cliff
    Taking a bend too fast, in Scotland.

It was ditched in a car park
    On Willesden Green.
So under the Civic Amenities Act 1967
    Section No. 20

Removal and Disposal of Abandoned Vehicles
    The Transport and Cleansing Division
Of the London Borough of Brent
    Will sell it for scrap.

Some other owner is responsible,
    The next sucker in the line.
But I feel tonight a remote sense of guilt
    Mixed with a tinge of outrage

To think of the rationality of that great engine
    Ripped into shreds,
The camshaft smashed, the radial tyres torn loose,
    And the little dancing horse stripped from the grill.

It had electric windows, in 1961.
        It had the original radio, with its aerial.
It could out-accelerate any car in Europe.
        They don't come off the floor like that any more.

Badger's Poem

The badger ran rapidly down the
        thick walk, snuffling.
Eee, eee, eee, he cried, when he stopped.

He was a good badger.

Very sleek were his incurved paws, and his
        lean snout.
His belly, very commodious.

He was a good eater, was this badger.
Worms, worms, and more worms.

His stomach was a veritable cauldron of worms.

Anyway, apart from that.

Why are you writing a poem about this little
        furry obnoxious badger?

He isn't obnoxious.

Oh? Well, they say he is.
Out west, they're killing him in hundreds.

With guns. With poison gas. With vicious dogs.
And (for all I know) with trained weasels.

Poor badger.
I wouldn't like to be him.

Even if I was as bad as they say he is.

I should expect a better deal.

So I'm putting this particular badger in a poem.
To commemorate his glossy appearance, and his
    neat nocturnal habits.

Very like in fact those of an English gentleman
    on his way to a dinner party.
The sort of English gentleman who is presently
    massacring his kind with dogs, etc.

Eee, eee, eee, he cried, when he stopped.
And I'll bet you would, too.

Last Night

I

Something that walked on air,
And curled in my chairs, has gone.
I saw its beautiful face
Grown lined with care and wan.

II

The poison was in its head,
I expect, before it came.
I never thought it could spread
And spoil our marvellous game.

III

It lived on silks, for a time.
It kept things in my drawers.
It would dig its nails in my skin.
Its ways were as sweet as a whore's.

IV

Its claws lay on my arm
As light as moss. It stirred,
And my air was what it breathed:
Its joy was what I heard.

V

It came to me in my room,
And it went, whenever it came.
Its long skin lay unrolled,
And that was always the same.

VI

Sometimes at dawn I would wake
And feel it warm on my back.
It had come close in the dark
Out of some sense of lack.

VII

And then, one October night
In an old house far away
I thought that I heard it cry,
And it wanted me to stay.

VIII

Outside the window I watched
The shapes of the oaks in the wind.
It was eating what it could,
But its flesh was wasted and thinned.

IX

Nothing could save it now,
Not even the taste of love.
I touched the infected flesh
That the long hair lay above.

X

It was all that I had to own.
Its fur was on all my sleeves.
I stooped, and kissed its face.
And it died, amidst the leaves.

To Weep

I ask the night sky, I ask the stars to weep.
I ask the hanging jackets in the bedroom cupboard
to weep.
I ask the filing cabinets in the little bedroom.
I ask the pot the fish is cooked in
in the kitchen to weep.
I ask the bowl of the lavatory.
I ask the porcelain of the hand-basin to weep.

II

I ask the remote dials in the dashboard of
the car to weep.
I ask the gutter.
I ask the snails in the long grass in
the park to weep.
I ask the black rabbit eloping with
her own shadow in the garden to weep.
I ask the toad.

III

I ask the darkness creeping out of the
ground to weep.
I ask the light.
I ask the pepper hinting at its own annihilation
in the sweet larder to weep.
I ask the sweating cheese.
I ask the spoons to weep.
I ask the delivered bottles of Glenfiddich
still wrapped in their Christmas cellophane.
I ask the milk to weep.

I ask the sheets, I ask the pillow to weep.
I ask the spider below the skirting-board.
I ask the chamber-pot to weep.
I ask the ceiling.
I ask the spectacles in their case to weep.
I ask the boots with their broken zip.

V

I ask the wilderness in the mind of
the pony going to the slaughter-house to weep.
I ask the blood raging.
I ask the solicitor with his gavel.
I ask the auctioneer on the chopping-block
to weep.
I ask the hangman selling knuckle-bones
to the proper authorities to weep.
I ask the skull.

The Place of Being

I

It had fallen in, or been broken.
The top was in angles of slabs
  That lay sideways, slightly askew.
I could see the bare earth underneath.

The metal holder for flowers
Had gone. But a small green moss
 Was growing in earth in the casing.
I touched it with my thumb.

On the scatter of chips of granite
Some little plant was blooming
 That might have been heather. The headstone
Was stained, darkened with soot.

II

It was cold in the wind on the hill,
But the view was quite beautiful.
 New buildings rose in the mist
In the valley, towers of concrete.

Somewhere down there, live people
Went about their autumn business,
 Forgetful of the dead in their graves.
As I had been, until now.

I stood for a moment with head bowed,
Wondering what to say.
 But I couldn't think of anything.
And it seemed stupid to kneel.

So I lifted a sycamore leaf
From the shallow drift on your bodies,
 And folded it into my pocket.
And then I walked away.

318

A Divorce Poem

I

That wooden sword I dreamed
  Several nights ago
Was the one my father made
  And wrapped in sticky tape
With vermilion paint on the blade

For blood. In my dream it was yours,
  The one you gripped in a fight
Against someone twice your size
  You had to beat for your life
And who got you between the eyes.

It was white and smooth, I remember,
  Curved like a scimitar
And with, somewhere, an awkward notch
  Like a bite out of a cake
Or the V in a woman's crotch.

II

Was that why? I wonder
  As I try to interpret the dream
Just why it sank, and then died,
  And then rose again the next night.
I suppose it may have implied

That this patriarchal sword
  Was a weapon I much admired
When, in fact, it had lain unused
  In a cupboard of soldiers and toys.
Years later, I grew confused.

With my forefinger and thumb
I would stroke the line of the tape
And the vague edge of the splash
Where the paint suggested blood
With a scatter of drops like a rash.

But I feel a black hilt in my hand
And a curved blade enter my groin
As I write, and I dream again
When you lay your glasses aside
That I strike with the strength of ten.

Breaking Up

It begins to slide. In the wake of the sun,
Soft as tar,
They feel its edges grow viscous. As if spun

Just too far
Towards their heat, it sucks back, seethes. Only now
It is too late. Gradually, a long spar,

Like an axe, shapes itself on one side. Where their plough
Creaks, trembles at the brink, it opens, reveals
Fissures. How

They both react to that understanding seals
Its first gash
In ripples. You might have thought scraping of wheels,

Or a flash,
Would have warned them before. It seems not. These two
Were too close. In the orbit of their slow crash

Its glister formed a narrowing echo. Through
Plains of white
Veils, acres of their tears froze. Folded, snow flew

On a flat circle, receding through twilight
In complete dulled thunder, so that neither heard
Ice-turn, bite

Of toothed hail, or a frost-manacle. All furred
Thoughts were toys
In the warmth of a knowing touch. If each word,

Shape, employs
An edge on them now, that was earned. So they glide
Together in a sort of code, a grave poise

As of corners wrongly skated. If a hide,
A fleece, were stretched, scented with pole-wind, that one,
Hung inside,

Would shake, shiver. This one, glassed like a flare-gun
Which can fire
Only in caves of ice, would wince. In the sun,

Then, they stand, but are split now. Their stiff beech-pyre
Is the cause
Of those incisions, that flowing. A wet spire

Of glass, floors
Of slip-ice, trouble its grip. It nudges bare
Outlets. They watch it crumble, turn as it soars,

Almost without crust, for a nook in the air
To be at ease in. As with a cooling star,
It must share,

In the gravity of its fall, what they are
Now, were before,
And have renewed. It cracks to a wound, a scar.

A Gift

Returning from the car, I come late home
And hear you weeping through the closed front door
Before the key scrapes in the lock. In the dark
I see you sitting, halfway up the stair,
Curled in a foetus-shape as though in a womb,
Wearing your dressing-gown, striped red and gold,
As if for a ceremony not to take place,
Dressed up for birth, and still not to be born.

There are no words to show how much I care.
I go downstairs, close the door in my brain
On what seems too terrible to let out
Though it rips inside me. And then outside
In the quiet garden, behind the house,
I hear another sound, a scraping by stealth.
Turning, I reach to let in what I can.
I bring you the soft new hedgehog in my hands.

In the Same Room

Rain falls. Trickling on the flat roof
Where we face towards the mountains. The lake

On the other side stretches calmly
In the darkness. And the sounds lovers make

As they go to bed together filter in
From the corridor. You lie and read

And I lie and read in the same room
With my back to you. Whatever we need

From each other still, it isn't sex,
Or not that exactly. Creaking of beds

Rarely took place in our world. I speak
Now, and we both turn our tired heads

And you say, sweetly and softly, good night.
And the rain goes on falling. And that feels right.

The Flame of Love, by Laura Stargleam

a Mills and Boon poem

I

Garth Symbel strode up the hill towards
the dark bulk of Lornewood Castle, grimly
silhouetted against the setting sun. The harsh

contours of his swarthy face were set in dour
lines as he thought back over what had happened
in the shadow of the dripping laurels earlier that

winter afternoon. Lorelei Fairstance was
a mere chit of a girl, but the tilt of her
little nose and the jut of her pretty hips

had been too much for the pent-up feelings
of Garth's wicked neighbour, Aldrich
Mindslade.

II

Garth gripped the horsewhip

tighter in his powerful fist as he burst through
the flanking bushes at the gates of the mansion. Yes,

the man was going to be taught a lesson be
would remember for a long while, Garth was sure
of that. 'Garth!' Lorelei was waiting

beside the old oak outside the narrow
Gothic windows of the conservatory. In the gathering
twilight, the moon shone lightly on the

324

waterfall of chestnut hair that fell over
her delicate shoulders, now partly exposed under
the straps of her Dior evening dress.

III

'Lorelei!'

Garth spoke with a touch of surprise. He
had not expected to meet his future bride
here before he had taught the would-be usurper

a lesson. 'I hadn't expected to see you out
so late. You'll catch your death of cold in
that light wrap. Here, let me cover

you up.' Lorelei moved away, drawing in her
breath with a touch of suppressed excitement to
feel his boldly male hand reach out for

the bare skin of her shoulder. 'Garth. No.' she
whispered. 'Not now.' She drew the shawl
tighter over herself, shrinking back against

the warm stone of the old castle wall.

IV

'Why,
Lorelei. You silly little girl. I'm not going
to hurt you. I worship the very ground you

tread upon. You know that. I'm here to
teach that scoundrel Aldrich Mindslade he can't
play around with your affections.' Lorelei

325

put her hand to her mouth. A little gasp
came out, as she heard Garth speak these fateful
words.

V

'O Garth. No,' she said. 'He

meant no harm. I promise you that. I
wonder if it wasn't half my own fault.' Garth
laughed shortly. 'Well, in that wisp of an

evening dress, I can understand how
you might think that,' he said. 'But the
man must be taught to control his passions. I

mean to give him a taste of this.' And
he cracked the horsewhip in the cool air.

VI

Lorelei
gave out a little cry. 'Garth. Garth.' she

whispered. 'Let him be. I beseech you.
No harm has been done yet by his folly, but
if you flog him now there will be

lasting feud between our houses.' Garth Symbel
frowned. He looked up at the castle towering away
to the moon. 'Maybe,' he said. 'But it can't

be helped.'

VII

At this moment the slim figure of Aldrich
Mindslade appeared round the corner of the house. Lorelei
screamed. It was going to be a bitter

confrontation. 'Mindslade,' said Garth. 'I
was looking for you. I'm going to teach you a
lesson you won't forget. Stand over there

by that old tree.'

VIII

'Symbel,' said Aldrich
Mindslade. 'I know what you're thinking. But
please don't judge me too harshly. I

love Lorelei and I mean to marry her. If
I was carried away today in the heat of passion,
I'm sorry. She knows that.' A dark

wave of anger swept across Garth Symbel's
handsome face, and his fingers clenched on
the stem of the whip. 'Marry her,' he

ground out. 'Why, you swine. You aren't fit
to sweep the grass she walks on. She's mine.
And never you forget it.'

IX

'Garth, oh Garth.'

Lorelei rushed forward and flung herself
madly into Garth Symbel's arms. 'I never
thought you cared. Why did you never say?

327

Oh Garth. Leave him alone, and kiss me.
Here. Now. In the garden. Do what you will!'
It was all that Garth could do to

hold in the rising tide of his passion. With
a curt gesture he motioned to Aldrich
Mindslade to leave them alone, and

the other man slunk off into the darkness.

X

By
the light of the moon Garth gazed down
into Lorelei's fair head on his

shoulder. He threw the whip aside. 'My
dear sweet little girl,' he said. 'Not
here. Not now. I want it to be so right

the very first time with you. And that
means when we're married. In a church.' The
rush of feeling was almost more than

Lorelei could stand.

XI

She felt her heart
pulsing under her thin straps. 'Oh yes, Garth,
yes,' she found herself saying. And

out beyond her in the sky the frail
moon seemed to sing like a bird as it
sailed over the battlements. And in

her heart joy spread its wings like a
dove and she knew that from now on
everything, everywhere, was always going to be all right.

328

By Way of a Prologue

I

Imagine, in England,
  Someone who is looking at the sun moving
    Through the dilapidated remnants
Of the eastern hemisphere. His name is Harry, but
      He is not, or is not yet,
  That insouciant, military progenitor
    Whom all will recall
From the history of Agincourt. He is Harry Crosby.

II

Imagine, gentlemen,
  That he has a pair of binoculars
    Constructed of good German glass
And that he is watching that red, singular orb
    With a kind of passion
  Most of us give only to women. He is utterly possessed
    With the magnificent, celestial
Burnish of the solar energy. He is Harry Crosby.

III

Imagine, in your mind's eye,
  Two people lying dead on a bed in
    A small ninth-floor room
In an uptown hotel in New York City. It is nineteen
      Twenty-nine
  And the stock market is about to crash, but
    That is not why the young man
With the smoking gun in his hand has fired. He is Harry Crosby.

IV

Imagine the winter sun
  Glittering through the forgotten window on the still
    Beautiful eyes
Of the girl he has killed by a shot in the brain
      Or who has perhaps
  Killed herself, we are not sure, by a shot
    Pre-arranged with him, or
Not pre-arranged, and has left him alive. He is Harry Crosby.

V

Imagine that just one second
  Ago the blood welled from a single wound in her head
    And the girl died
In the path of the sun driving across Manhattan
    Towards a new decade
  And imagine that Harry Crosby who has been
    In love with her, as with many others,
Has taken the last light on his shaking brow. And the play is
about to begin.

VI

Imagine that somewhere in Heaven
  The nationality of catastrophe has become incidental
    And that Harry Crosby
Is a myth of England. Yes, it seems different now,
    I know, to be imagining
  Someone so close to home on that lonely bed
    In the winter light
With a head wound. With a terrible sickness of the heart.

Imagine, perhaps, though,
That the sickness for which this improbable hero died
Was a little thing
No larger than the tiny crozier in a woman's forks
For which the sun stooped
Out of the black sky, and sold his name.
Imagine that Harry Crosby
Lifted his heart, and the sun took it. And he was you.

Two Days After

When we lay down, I touched
Your breasts, and they were wet
With something white.
I asked you, and you clutched
Your silk shirt tight.
It brushed me. And I let

Your hand stray down, and pluck
At the blood below my jeans.
Your eyes were bold.
You wanted me to fuck,
And I was cold.
It seemed the future's means

Lay in that darkening stain
Where everything had stuck.
Your eyes grew mild.

331

You beckoned me to suck
  Milk for our child
While death was still in flood.

  That night, as if in prayer,
  I entered you behind
With, I suppose, some pride
  In having you so bare
  Of what was in your mind,
Or what had grown inside.

  This lay now far away
  Unfettered, and untried,
And, perhaps, at rest.
  I came. And then I cried.
  And that seemed best,
I thought I heard you say.

A Poem for Breathing

  Trudging through drifts along the hedge, we
Probe at the flecked, white essence with sticks. Across
    The hill field, mushroom-brown in
  The sun, the mass of the sheep trundle
As though on small wheels. With a jerk, the farmer

  Speaks, quietly pleased. *Here's one*. And we
Hunch round while he digs. Dry snow flies like castor
    Sugar from the jabbing edge

332

Of the spade. The head rubs clear first, a
Yellow cone with eyes. The farmer leans, panting,

On the haft. *Will you grab him from the
Front?* I reach down, grope for greasy fur, rough, neat
    Ears. I grip at shoulders, while
  He heaves at the coarse, hairy
Backside. With a clumsy lug, it's up, scrambling

For a hold on the white, soft grass. It
Stares round, astonished to be alive. Then it
    Runs, like a rug on legs, to
  Join the shy others. Ten dark little
Pellets of dung steam in the hole, where it lay

Dumped, and sank in. *You have to probe with
The pole along the line of the rest of the
    Hedge. They tend to be close.* We
  Probe, floundering in Wellingtons, breath
Rasping hard in the cold. The released one is

All right. He has found his pen in the
Sun. I dig in the spade's thin haft, close to barbed
    Wire. Someone else speaks. *Here's
  Another.* And it starts again. The
Rush to see, the leaning sense of hush, and the

Snow-flutter as we grasp for the quick
Life buried in the ivory ground. *There were
    Ninety-eight, and I counted
  Ninety-five.* That means one more. And I
Kneel to my spade, feeling the chill seep through my

Boots. The sun burns dark. I imagine
The cold-worn ears, the legs bunched in the foetus

Position for warmth. I smell
The feathery, stale white duvet, the
Hot air from the nostrils, burning upwards. And

I crouch above the sheep, hunched in its
Briar bunk below the hedge. From the field, it
Hears the bleat of its friends, their
Far joy. It feels only the cushions
Of frost on its frozen back. I breathe, slowly.

Trying to melt that hard-packed snow. I
Breathe, melting a little snow with my breath. If
Everyone in the whole
World would breathe here, it might help. Breathe
Here a little, as you read, it might still help.

The Creed

I

One day, perhaps, I shall die
In some foreign guerrilla war.
That's what it all seems for,
I think, sometimes, in my dreams.
I use the word dreams for hopes,
Or fears, or for my ideals,
Not for what happens in bed.
One day I shall be out there dead,
One mote in the terrible fire,
As if I had never been.

334

I have no fear of that.
I shall blink in the eye of the cat
The Egyptians thought the sun was.
Bravery comes in the night,
I suppose, the three o'clock kind,
When you wake, half drunk, as I have,
Rising for water, or juice,
With your head in a dizzy whirl,
And thinking about your girl.
Well, the long night has its use
When it forces me into this
In lieu of sex, or a kiss.

II

Alive still at forty-six,
What do I care about?
I don't know, I really don't know.
But I feel what I feel, I know that.
Nobody can take away
Those creatures that watch in fur
I give life to, who give me life,
The gods, and toys, of my brain.
If they circle, they always return
To keep me safe while I sleep.
You can laugh, laugh if you dare.
Nothing matters but faith
To what matters inside the heart.
Write that down for a start.
I believe in the stress of the world,
In the insurgency of pain
That will go, and will come again.
We are under perpetual siege
By the powers of darkness. Yes,
And I'd have it no other way,

335

Child of that sluggish war,
As I am, that will never die.
There will always be bombers there
At the back of my burning head,
And my father in uniform.
I have no time for progress, or luck.
Sometimes it seems as if
I hunt at each party with claws,
I reach out for love with my teeth.
I go up when I hear the alarm,
Scrambled in fur in the cold.
With the dawn air on my chin,
They come into my sights at speed
And my body moves out to kill.
The enemy. No, the friends
I have to have or I die.

III

I feel colder now as I write,
And the alarm clock ticks up towards five.
Outside through the sash I can see
The light blue-green of the day.
I want to address this to you.
I need your name, at the end,
To make sense of the bitterness,
The rage, and the words in place.
You give me the force to write
As directly and flat as I've done.
I take energy out of your face
With my eyes. Off your skin
With my hands. Through your blood
By the penetration of love.
It needn't always be you.
I know, and I fear it won't.

It wasn't before, and I felt
The same as I do tonight.
But it's you today. And I feel
The intensity of it break
Into simple, clear-cut thoughts.
We think the same. You believe
In what I believe, a bit.
More than others do, you trust
In the myth of being brave.
I love you for that. And I will,
Even if things go wrong.
At least, I hope that I will,
And I hope that they won't tonight.
You're asleep with another man.
I trust you, and why you are,
And I trust you in loving me.
Trust here, perhaps, is hope.
I suppose only that. And yet
What else is there now, as I end,
With the blue-green growing grey,
And the sour taste of your drink
In my throat, and the need to sleep
Long gone, and another day
Out there to live in and deal with,
And three more until we meet?

Somewhere

In all those rooms, no light
Unfiltered by the trees.
Only the broken spears
Of sunlight through smudged glass:
And windows dimmed with webs.

Across the road, thin sheep
And a church behind its yews.
Weeds to a crumbled wall
And an undergrowth of grass
Great roots of beech lay bare.

Indoors, the musty smell
Of old wood drying through
And forgotten food left out.
Sour milk in open cups.
Dead bread along a board.

There are many beds unmade
In that exotic house.
The remains of passengers
Whose lives have fallen in
And thrown them out to the sky.

In the attics, time has knelt
And driven holes through jars.
The scum of paint in tins
Tells of a former care
That blistered in the halls.

A foot of green slime swills
In the cellar by the stairs.

Brick arches built for wine
Are in water to their knees
And toads now croak for port.

Here, on the barren floors,
The vapid slap of soles
Remainders gaiety
To the drone of testy flies.
Even the cat's foot slurs

In unfurnished corridors
And the hinges of the doors
Creak with a hidden weight.
There is black, unmanaged soot
On the ostrich of each grate.

Whoever used these rooms
Has abandoned them to the air.
Air, and the stink of rats.
But outside, the long gallery
Of chestnuts rustles leaves

And the garden gives away
What the mansion chose to lose,
A sense of grand repose.
The stately lines of pride
From a rectitude of prayer

Are simplified to the shape
Of a summer's afternoon
Where growth is an elegance
And people come to read
In the shadow of old trees.

Walking, and loving these,
Is the gentle wind and the heat,
May be all that remains to aid
Or obliterate the decay.
It seems so, this summer's day.

The Flyers

In the bad days I had five animals, five toys.
An owl made of red tufts, an owl with brown wings, a
      little white owl, and an owl made by the Society
          for Distressed Gentlefolk,
and a dog, a Skye terrier, whose name was Dougal.

Why these, I never knew.
But they flew.

Night after night round Richmond in the dark, for
      fun, and to take care of things.

But if I needed them, they were back.
I never knew them gone, or saw them landing, and was
      frightened by it.

They were always there, staring out it seemed into
      the lighted streets, from the window sill.

Every night I came home at two in the morning, quiet
      and guilty, I arranged those five totemic apologies
         on their sill.
Every morning they were there, to be seen.

Sometimes, even, she woke in the half-darkness, and
    murmured,
    happy it seemed and sleepy, *the flyers*.

And that was enough.
Just enough, in the bad days, to keep the world going.

This morning, after what she and I never had, or rarely,
    sexual intercourse, you said you could see a badger
        outside in the field, through the window.
Joking, to wake me up.

I said the little badger, the fur one who lies all
    day on our bed, went outdoors at times, but
      we never saw.

It brought them back.
The flyers, and what they meant.

I write these lines here as you take your bath, alone
    now for only a moment, sad for what never was.

Commemorating the flyers.

Five Horse Chestnuts

    I saw them shine. They were the first,
    This cooling year, thrown hard and bland
Along the littered road in Pembridge Square,
    Amidst the pointed leaves. And there,

341

Caught by the sunlight, on my open hand,
I felt their power, with a kind of thirst.

    It comes in colour. Then in sheen
      And polish, to impair, and move,
Part plausible as elegance, or age,
    A kind of rich, hand-crafted rage
For keeping living to some furnished groove,
And, more, for being ripe now. Now I lean

    Their five shaped honest backs to rest
      Along your rosewood writing-desk
We bought in Hampstead. And its brass knobs, bright
    Although near winter, take the light
Out of the foolish west. And, Hardyesque
In gloomy sun, like nipples on a chest,

    They throw the gleams back. I salute
      Such loyal redness, glowing down.
Times changed for us, and nights grew darker. Yes,
    When I screwed tight my trouser-press,
One night, beside you, in your dressing-gown,
Our ailments verged on autumn, and bore fruit.

    You filed your suit. And I drew back,
      And, in that drawing, found relief
From what was mine. My illness, or my guilt,
    Never expired on what we built,
Nor even from the fungus of your grief
That ate through reason. Like a kind of lack,

    It fed on dying, and prepared its price,
      In sores that festered later. Well,
It had its parallel, for me, with what
    I knew before, my war-bred knot

Untieable by trying. Truth to tell,
I think all loved ones die, but mine die twice,

And stain my mind. Things grow too plain.
I leave my shelled nuts for you, sure
Of your approval of their glowing needs,
Their polished rounds, their glittering seeds,
Their purpose to create, and to endure.
Through dying leaves, and shells, to bloom again.

It would be so for me. The power
That, rising, settles from the tree
And scatters uncupped energies. That, white
Through thawing soil, emerges light
And flexible, as branches. This, for me,
Is what I wait for, through each wasted hour,

In hope. The power still to smile
Through days of dimming to the dark
Where dreams and absence violate the brain,
And vex its cadence. To retain,
From all those flowering chestnuts in the park,
One branch of sticky buds, transformed by style.

Their Flying Dreams

Today you piled a barrow high with bricks,
And cleared the grate, and lit a blazing fire.
Beside your flames, we stretched our cracking hands,
And hunched in sheepskin. And I felt at home.

343

Outside, our gutters may have harboured leaves,
And muddy rain replaced the promised snow.
But here, beneath each stone Victorian rose,
I spread my booted legs, and felt a lord.

In the empty library, I saw my books
Rise in their rosewood case, and stoop from shelves.
Urns over walnut watched the distant yews
And shutters marked the floorward swoop of glass.

Time would remove this dusty patina
From boards no longer young, but still laid true.
And space would shrink the measured stretch of pine
To something darker, to a table's glare.

I warmed, and rose, and walked towards the wall.
Shaking the curtain loose from its brass rings,
I took the thinning cloth. And then a moth,
A huge one, with four hawk's heads, rose and flew.

It hit the window like a wetted sheet,
It seemed, until I loosened the glass catch,
And let it through. It flew towards the south,
Into what sun was left, and left me safe.

It seemed an omen. I could live and work
In these firm rooms, and shake them loose of life
Into the burst world, if I wanted, free
To shatter daylight, and leave me my dues.

Air to the winged things, and to me my house.
A proper bargain. And the slackening rain
Seemed for a moment to admit more light
Out of your fire, to confirm this bond.

I saw the future, and our children stand
Mirrored against those blackened, further trees
In the cold December night: and, hand in hand,
At ease with us, gather their flying dreams.

Katrine's Kittens

Behind the fire-guard, against a spade,
Near to a green tray, in the inglenook,
By a bellows, and an iron, they were laid.
I heard their tiny mewling. And I took
A pair of cushions to make bricks more kind,
And propped her back. But she was of no mind

For luxury, or sloth. She licked the head
Of one just born, and purred. Thus reassured
By that huge rumbling, he looked much less dead,
And raised his blind eyes, and was black, and cured.
They were five now. Like mice against her side,
Mouths to her nipples. And not one had died.

I turned, and smiled at you. Life had begun
For another handful, on a day of blue
And cloud-flecked sky, in the September sun,
And these were Librans, mutable like you.
The mother moved round, and I watched her rest,
Five small heads heaving on her tired breast.

You turned away to type, and I to write,
And the morning darkened. By the ancient bricks,

Turning to check, I saw another sight,
A mass of jelly. And I counted six.
The sixth small kitten came too late, and cold,
And needed help. When he was one hour old,

You warmed him in a duster. By the sink,
Along the Aga, cleaned his mucused nose,
And felt him stir. A sudden mouth, round, pink
And raw, opened, and then his high voice rose,
And yelled for help. Hours later, now, I say,
Six kittens are alive still, born today.

One Gone, Eight to Go

On a night of savage frost,
This year, my smallest cat,
The fluffy one, got lost.
And I thought that that was that.

Until, late home, I heard,
As I fumbled for my key,
The weak sound of some bird.
He was there, mewing to me.

There, on the icy sill,
Lifting his crusted head,
He looked far worse than ill.
He looked, I'd say, quite dead.

Indoors, though, he could eat,
As he showed, and fluffed his tail.

So much for a plate of meat.
So much for a storm of hail.

Now, by the burning grate,
I stroke his fragile spine,
Thinking of time, and fate.
Lives go. Men don't have nine,

As kittens do, to waste.
This lucky one survives,
And purrs, affronted-faced.
But even he, who thrives

Tonight, in my cupped hands,
And will grow big and grey,
Will sense, in time, the sands,
And fail, and shrink away.

Thoughts on a Box of Razors

bought at a Stalham sale

I

For two pounds, they were mine. The price seemed right.
I thought of Housman's shiver, as he shaved,
And open sorrows that might cut the skin.

One razor curves beside me, black and clean.
It seems to swoop, when closed, as though in flight.

347

The hollow, bird's-beak-sectioned blade's engraved.
I touch its coldness, anxious to begin,

Watching the thirteen others as they grin.
Men's tender bodies are what razors craved.
I sense their famished hunger, their sweet bite,
Their glitter in ebony, obsessed, obscene.

And yet this glitter, with its power to stun
That seems so Japanese in these, looks trite.
It takes me back to Sheffield, and what's done.

II

Suppose I try to focus on just one.
This German GBNG, flecked with rust
And dated 1918, 's caught the sun.
Spread out across my page, its vague V-thrust

And hooking nose bring Dorniers to mind.
My war, that was. I hear old engines drone,
And civilians dying, with no testament signed.
That blitz was mine, I feel it as my own.

Others have carried razors, cold like this,
And stropped them sharper on strong leather thongs.
I touch my German friend. Its rustling kiss
Across my finger thrills like Chinese gongs.

I see the owner was E. Mann, my name.
My mother had one like this, much the same.

III

I go too far. I've jammed one in a churn,
A butler's cleaner for a carving-knife.

348

You shove a handle, and twinned rollers turn
And clear the blades of grease. In all my life

I never saw one till eight months ago
At an Aylsham sale. I bought the next I saw,
And cleaned it up. I use it now with dust
Of emery powder that's already in.

It's weak, but it works, with knives. A kind of crust
Will come off surfaces, and make things show.
I thought I'd clear the razor of some flaw,
But it caught inside. The blades of knives are thin,

A razor's upper section's far too thick.
This made the movement of that whole drum stick.

IV

Now I lay ten in a circle. Each has teeth,
Like cogs in an alarm-clock, and a groove.
As if relaxing, edges are in sheath,
And out of sight. They make a ring of steel,

Whose rim is ivory, whose hub is bills,
Or beaks. I mean the hooks you shift them by,
And make their sharkness arch with. As it moves,
You feel the irony. It eats and chills.

The irony that glisters in each eye,
Brassy and raised, is part of why they wheel
Into such penguin swimming forms. They fly
Only when open, vicious by the keel

That clears by inches the sea floor of time,
And leaves for grief deposits, bloody slime.

349

'Napoleon' seems much skinnier than the rest.
A trifle stiff-backed, and a smidgeon marred.
In the middle of his blade, he has a nick.
Old Nick. They might have called him that, for fun,
In Sheffield, England, where they carved his kind,
Those cutler brothers, John and William Ragg.

I see them in their sweat-shop, bony crags
Like stalwart men, with Elba on their mind.
They slaved, like Mr Stokes, like everyone
Who listened for the cold alarm-bell's click,
And took home hands grown calloused, and bone-hard.

These built Napoleon, by their chimney-breast,
And sent him far from Sheffield, to shave chins.
I tap their dread invention on my shins.

VI

Razors need razor-like precision. These
Don't quite have that. This boxful leans on rhyme.
I see the brook of recollection freeze,
And feel the cross of parting, like a crime.

I could abandon rhyme, though. Force a sly
Sixth-line decision to be less exact.
A sort of gear change, as it were, in fact.
That would be fluid, like a flow of thigh.

I don't suppose I'll do it, though, nor try.
Good rhymes can cut you. They can make you cry.

Remembering does that, too. So when I
Remember blue Gillette, and rusting blades,

A kind of guilty subjugation shades.
I see my father's car, and cases packed.

VII

Wearing these memories, in their common flight,
I take up three fresh razors, heavy ones,
All black. I need the heft of weight tonight,
The drag of solid iron, like a plough's,

To upheave my brain. Ideas hinge and flee
At the solstice of a poem. They earn space
By how they touch me. Seconds out, I see
The reaching hands of grief, and her blank face.

The razors wait like rifles, nose to tail.
Like strips of hardened sword-blade, in a pail.
Like knights in armour, for their holy grail
Going to war, in coats of khaki mail.

Turning, I hear the sound of English guns.
I see my mother's tears. I touch her blouse.

VIII

I touched her blouse again when she was ill,
Feeling the curve. Razors have that, well wound
As if around some foreign hill. Great scythes
Don't hold the same allure. Scythes rake the ground

While razors float. They take our skin for tithes,
Winged surgeons. At our faces, with their fists,
They scrape and till, until the tissue breaks,
And leaves wide acres open to bare cysts.

351

The mother's curve, though. Is it this that makes
The elegance of swords from old Japan?
The simple shape of Time, drawn as a man?

I don't know. There's a straightness in their rule,
Razors. When I was nearly twelve, at school,
I used to want a razor that would kill.

IX

I never got one, though. I bought my first
At a garage sale in Saratoga Springs.
It's lying stiff, bone-yellow, much the worst
For wear, while all my rest make rings

Around it, on that empty cabinet
Whose lacquer top I'm using for their ground.
It's ominous, a tale of warring kings,
A nightmare game. How ten bright shiners rose

And trapped a colleague on their killing-mound.
Somehow I don't suppose the rest would set
Into a pattern slighter than I chose
If any sliced his neighbour into bits

And screeched away. I wonder, though, if it's
More razor-like to savage with no sound?

X

Once you get fantasy, what's left to say?
You get sheer viciousness, a misty sheen.
Imagine some girl murderously neat,
Stiff as a fish-bone sticking in your throat.

She takes a sharpened razor. To make sure,
She sharpens pencils. To make doubly sure,
Until those hexagons shed flakes of cones
She sharpens. Those are fir-tree's, these are hers.

She sees her man walk home from Stalham, gay
In his gaiety, and randy as a stoat.
It isn't easy to be quite so mean,
Even as she is, like a bitch on heat.

She does it, though. Cover the man with stones.
Bury this John Clarke's razor, with his bones.

XI

No true disciple of the modern world
Would aim to buy a cut-throat still to use.
Even a safety razor might seem odd.
Those brushes in the window, that arcade

Off Piccadilly, seem to stand for show.
Collectors might accept one, nicely curled
Into a smooth maroon case. Years ago
When all men lathered, in some louche decade,

It might have frightened you to read the news
Of a Sweeney Todd, a-swivel in your chair.
It wouldn't quite have marked one as a clod
Not to be shaved well, but, in good repair,

A gentleman kept razors. That was life.
As necessary as a decent wife.

XII

My father lost his, in a time of strife,
Long after he had gone. In middle age
My mother knew the worst, and what she said
Stays with me now. The Royal Hospital

Had instruments laid out on moving trays,
Like razors. Did they shave the nightly dead,
And lay them empty in each well-made bed?
This is the memory that slowly slays,

The sight of screens. What happens with the knife
Behind those frills must happen to us all
In years to come. And it's good cause for rage,
That frictive rage against the dying light

I feel seep through these handled, broken forms,
And rake in agony, like icy storms.

XIII

Downstairs I hear the heater moving. Tired,
I know it's after eight, and time to eat.

You will be cooking, standing by the stove,
Slicing potatoes, carrots, from your crate.
The table may be laid. And silvered blades,
Planted for eating, ordered by each plate.

They'll take my mind away from these retired
And scandalous old razors. Quite as neat
As razors, in much straighter lines, knives store
Bold energies of peace, of summoned awe

Our quiet house provides. By natural law
I ought to honour this deliberate grove

Of stainless trees. But, no. Knives have it made.
I prefer razors, they do rougher trade.

XIV

In sadness, I feel inspiration fail.
I bought these cut-throat razors in a box
With a wireless, and a metal case for coins.

I didn't need them, I just like old blades,
And things to keep things in, symbols of loins
Psychiatrists would say, the spike and hole.

But it's really more than that. I like these locks
Along the money-case, and on my chests,
Even if they don't close. I like the shocks,
The tingling brinks, of razors. In this house,
I falter sometimes when I touch your breasts.

I have to try again. To keep things whole,
In all we do, it helps to think of raids,
And live with a Sheffield edge. Wholeness is frail.

The Renewal

The need to find a place always returns.
In Richmond, where my eighteenth-century bricks
Fashioned an avenue to stable skin,

355

I built a proper house. At Holland Park,
That fleece and leather took their comfort from,
I tried another, in another way.

Both worked. And what the simple martyrdom
Of wanting some position broke for sticks,
And set in place, held back the creeping dark.

I turned there, in my darkness, on my beds,
In tiny rooms, alone, and with my wives,
Or girls who passed for wives. And all my burns

From being lonely, and unsatisfied,
Flared in the silence, like a sheen from tin.
I waited, and, while waiting, something died.

Then, in the heat of Norfolk, I found you.
You brought the sun, through darkness, to my hives,
The bolted iron to my crumbling sheds,

You changed the whole world's shape. Your power grew,
And I, in feeling that, wanted some place
More generous for it than those gentle homes.

I needed somewhere with a flirt of grace
To match your fervour for long acreage.
I found it, here at Oby. Naked space

Over the cornfields, and the next-door farm,
Contracts to an oasis with great trees
That north-east winds can ravage in their rage

And leave still rooted and serene. In these
I feel the sweep of beech-wood, like an arm,
And something deeper, in our copper beech.

That brings a birthright in its massive reach,
A sense of giant time. Seeing it blaze
In widespread feathering, I feel the past,

The creak of longships on the Caister shore,
The swing of mills beside the easy broads,
And something closer, groping slow, at last,

The pleasant rectors, knocking croquet balls.
I take their heritage, and what it pays,
And vow today to make its profits pour

Through founded channels, in my well-kept grounds,
As growth, and preservation. Nothing falls
Or sings, in this wide garden, but its sounds

Calm me, and make our full liaison rich.
So my dream-Scotland grief was noble in
Will drag its graves beneath these grounded urns,

And stake its base in watered Norfolk clay,
And Kinburn be reborn, as what it was,
And my grandfather, and our Springer bitch,

Both live, in their own way, and like it here,
And feel the rain and sunlight on their skin,
And no one tell apart, which one is which,

The dream of former grandeur, and the firm
Everyday presence of our daily lives.
This is my hope, and what these lines affirm.

A Letter to Lisa

It might have been a pack of cigarettes,
A matchbox, or a flattened envelope.
It isn't what it was, that gently sets
And focuses. It isn't that, I hope.

Others have written words on wrinkled tin,
On prison walls, on lavatory tiles.
A few have scattered fragments in a bin,
Or paged their anguish into gathered files.

I know one girl who burned her grief on skin,
And laid her agony in patterned smiles.
It isn't what it was, or what it's in,
Or where it goes, that shadows, and beguiles

In broken words, in cries for cancelled debts,
In open wounds where tempered feelings grope.
It isn't those. Not always. Not the pets
Of pampered vehicles that cringe to cope.

Others have chosen those. You took some card,
Just any card your tear-flushed eyeball scanned,
And bent your crayon to what seemed most marred
And least available to understand,

Your need. And yet your hint of suicide,
I wish that I can kill myself, seems less
Than what you pencilled on the other side:
The underbelly of your bitterness.

Oh, I can write these lines in decent pride,
And not feel too much sense of pain, and mess.

After all, children have been known to hide,
Even to denigrate, their happiness.

I wonder, though. It takes a heart too hard
For any praise of mine to find quite bland
I want to go back to my Daddy, starred
And blotted by a seven-year-old hand.

Spirits

Watching the window into the future
Which is Television,
In a cooled Edwardian room,

I heard one cry, in the distance,
Like a thin blade sticking in wood
Or a rusty hinge.

For a long time
I listened, wondering if I dared
Go out into the darkness

And look for it. At twilight,
I had seen several swoop
Like anchors, out of the eaves.

And once
I had halted, faced by an Austrian eagle
Hovering black on grey a foot or two from my eyes.

I went into the dairy
And out with a blue torch
Towards the beech-wood, in the east,

Where the sound came from.
It was louder there
In the night. A kind of frenzied sawing.

A few feet down
In the ha-ha
I flashed the beam into the branches.

But nothing moved.
Nothing except the grey kitten
Who had followed me out.

I went in, disappointed
And still afraid. I could have gone further
Into the blackness,

Called their name.
Instead, I came indoors
And sat down at the kitchen table,

Beating, you said,
The devil's tattoo, unconsciously,
On the scrubbed pine.

To Preserve Figs

for Iseult

Go up the whitewashed ladder, by the wall,
        And you'll find seven pounds
    Of them, half-ripened, on the tree.
            The rest were low
    I picked before. They wallowed free
            Near to the ground's
Welter of nettles, apples, weeds. I know,
    You'll have to take care. You might fall.

But there are plenty, seven pounds I'd say,
        Still floundering heavy, green
    And solid in the August air,
            And you can reach
    Them if you climb. So go up there
            And get them, keen
As fig-juice in your envy. Gather each
    Into your fingers, let none stay,

On the branch. It makes a metaphor for lust,
        This grasping for the rounds
    Of unripe figs that ooze their juice,
            Their sperm. It burns,
    That juice, and has no helpful use.
            You'll live with mounds
Of severed energy, with jaded urns
    Whose milked white necks you'll have to trust

Through all your life. It's best you learn that soon.
        The acid in the fruit
    Prickles the world with its pain

And nothing breaks
The dour addiction of the brain
To what may suit,
Or spoil. So watch your mother while she makes
These tractable. Take up a spoon

And help. Three times they boil, and have to steep,
Then boil again. Three times
It always has to be. So let
Them dry in trays
In your burning oven. Go and get
A sugary slime's
Blandishing oil. In winter, black to your gaze,
Like whales from arctic ice, they'll leap.

The Field, Tomorrow

I wanted the bare field out there to be mine.
Each day, at my typing, I saw the smooth line

Of the sycamores, breaking the sweep of the grass
To the farm and the river. I saw the sails pass

Far away, white and simple, where yachts moved at Thurne.
And I looked down, in pride, at my nearest stone urn.

From that urn to the sycamores, this was my land,
With the wide breadth of Norfolk stretched gold on each hand.

I had space, in my dream, and six acres to keep.
I had grass for my garden, and twenty new sheep.

It's all over. The field has been sold, to my friends,
And the dream of broad acres, all hope of it, ends.

At the auction I bid high, too high for my good,
And I'm glad that I missed it, at that price. I should

Have been forced into borrowing, bound to the shape
Of solicitor's ropes. But it still feels like rape

To see horses, brown horses, that other men own
(In my mind they seem galloping, sculptured like stone)

Out there in my bare field. I touch them, and weep,
And remember my dream, and the slow-moving sheep,

Their cold, lovely fleece, and their beautiful eyes,
And their mouths, low and cropping, surrounded by flies.

The Hornet

October brought the last one of the year
And laid it sleeping on your window-frame.
It stood for winter, and the failing game,
The end of something, and death coming near.

Drowned in a jug, with cardboard slid across
To keep it under, it sleeps always now,
Its warrior's head bent sideways, like a bow
Made to an enemy, for the mortal loss.

I see its body, simple as a cone
Of pine or Douglas fir, cypress or spruce.
It has no meaning, scarcely any use
Except to make more precious all we own,

The last of life, and living in this place,
Year in, year out, with what we have and hold,
Great barns, and trees, and somewhere to grow cold
And die in, when the time comes, with some grace

And a kind of honour, free from bitterness
Or rancour, and not losing elegance
At the last, as this dead hornet's final chance
Left it a scoop of terror. That, oh yes.

November at the Piano

for my mother

Not able to play, I touch your keys with the unskilled tips of
    my fingers, feeling a tune. The music
Echoes to the edge of the world. From the kitchen, the smell
    of a good dinner prowls, encountering my nose.

All senses coagulate. Holding the yellowed strips of ivory
    down, I squeeze out a last
Resonance from the hammered strings. It sings like a dying
    fly into corners of dust where vases

Of laurel abandon their petals. The delicate flavour of
    chord upon discord settles. The savour of hope

And melancholy in the balance of high and low that is all I
    can manage mingles. Outside the long window,

November is gathering force. In the sweat of the gale, my
    great beech-tree is sewing the grass with fire. I dwindle
Into another mould, a minute excrescence of tiny sound as I
    plunge my finger onto

A sharp note, slicing it off, like a breath of onion, or dry
    smoke. I remember your hands
As I touched them once, over sinks and baking bowls, and in
    power along such keys as these. I salute

Your competence in my ignorant feeling. I use my nose and
    my ears, under my hands, to arouse my mind.
I shall never play the piano, as you could play it, or cook,
    as you could cook. I can only

Suffer the sense of trying, hearing the sound, smelling the
    odour. This first November here
In my chosen Norfolk, what seems to matter is to ground
    your place in my echoing house, and to blaze your skills.

Mother, I need to remember, I need to feel. I have only these
    three senses to reach and hold
You with. Let me see your face in the fallen leaves. Let me
    taste your blood in the apples down from our trees.

Draft for an Ancestor

When I was young, and wrote about him first,
My Uncle Hugh was easier to hold.
      Now, in my age, at worst
    I take him by some outer fold
Of what was his. His Humber, by the door.
    That, at the least, if nothing more

Creates an image of his prosperous time
And thumbs in waistcoats to suggest their power.
      I hear tall glasses chime
    And clocks from walnut sound the hour
As they drive to Derby, where their horse will lose.
    At last, it seems, men have to choose

What traits in relatives they will to raise
To the height of models, awkward, fey, or strong,
      And there arrange as praise
    For the unhooked soul, keen to belong
To its family, some tree of love and grace
    In which there blossoms no mean face.

I feel this drive. As years go by, it grows
And I want an ancestry of heroic mould
      Fit for a world that knows
    How to accept the subtly bold
Who grasp at shields and leaves with a sprig of wit
    And honours their effrontery with it.

So Uncle Hugh, that self-made, stubborn man
I see in photographs, and hear in my head,
      Provides a flash of élan
    To the ranks of my more sombre dead

And, startling, floods their quarters with his brash
    And flighty Scottish kind of dash.

The Closet

for Joanna, before the cancer operation

This little closet, where I come to pray
    And read, is where I ought to sit
        And write, not kneel.

    I like the barrenness of it.
        It makes me feel
Monk-like, and I can sometimes be that way.

        It has two rooms.
    The outer one fronts on a yard
With a fine view of grass, urns and an ash.

    The chair I put in there, though hard,
        Seems rich and brash,
The jug and bowl cold marble, like a tomb's.

        But, through the door
Of simple sycamore, the rusting latch
    Creaks onto whitewashed walls,

        Odours that catch
    The breath, and something subtler, more
Like history's own air, that roughly shawls.

The window there,
High up, looks over nothing, it's opaque.
The floor is common brick, but cold.

It might look sad and bare,
Somewhere to void the intestine's inner fold,
Or stow a rake.

Once it was potting-shed. Once where
Men eased their bowels
Under that lively, fitted bench of pine:

A place for trowels
And bulbs, things moist and quaint and spare,
And now a sort of oratory, of mine.

I have a book,
A kind of altar, panelled seat, or splat,
Raised from a bedstead, gold and high

(Oddly pre-Raphaelite, at that)
And candles. I
Suppose I liked the Oxford Movement look

Their kind of tapering purple gave
To the narrow space
At noon: and something more, their light at night.

I made my nave,
Anyway, in this icy inner place
Run west: and that seemed almost right.

A sort of decorator's game
It was, at first,
And then a portent, now a kind of need.

Each day I go, and, in the name
Of some compulsion deeper than a creed,
      Think of the worst,

And even force my hands to hold
Each other in the shape for asking aid,
      And, from the floor

Beneath my legs, feel earthy cold
Creep up through tweeded flesh, and elbows laid
      On elm rubbed sore.

      Tonight, not there
But in the house, alone, as it grows dark,
      I hear the Easter Sunday wind

      Howl in the bare
Thin April beeches, feeling I have sinned.
      And what seems huge, and dim, and stark.

Is you still downstairs here, too ill
To see all this as mattering: fearful, soon
      To be in pain

Perhaps: or rise and live again,
Grateful for these ten days, as for a boon,
      But waiting, still.

A Cancer Ward

There was a lady, in another bed,
Older than you, who, when the mood would come
Moved her right hand across her brow, and then
Moved her left hand across her brow, and then
Moved her right hand across her brow, as if
        Brushing her hair.

Those knotty fingers reaching for her head
Are what remain: but, more than those, the sum
She counted as she moved her hands, and when
She'd finished counting, started up again,
Whipping her few white strands into a quiff
        Whose skull was bare.

And does it matter when you're so near dead
To grope for simple signals? To be dumb
Except for childhood maths: remembering men,
And how to add small digits, eight, nine, ten,
Cracking your knuckles where the joints are stiff
        And free to care

About what someone, years ago, once said
When drinks were mixed with light Jamaica rum,
And there were tram-cars, and you heard Big Ben
Out of the wireless, and you took your pen
And wrote your thank-you letters on the cliff
        Out in the air.

'Nanny says you must brush, wish to be wed,
And never bother if your arm grows numb.
Husbands don't grow like rushes in our fen.
You have to brush, smell nice: and, from their den,
The men will come, like badgers, to the whiff
        Of scented hair.'

The Last Bridge

for Joanna

To lie there on an iron bed,
Far from the world and all its care,
Surrounded by the nearly dead,
With death near, festering in the air,

To draw the slow stench up your nose
Of what may worsen, and grow stale,
Until you no more breathe than those
Who only breathe to feel they ail,

To hear the echo of a time
When something happened, like a sound
Of generous trumpets, fouled with slime,
That left you stranded in the ground,

To see the sky, outside your ward
Soiled by the yellow drift of rain,
False rain, unreal rain, and poured
Out of the jug that's grown your brain,

371

To clutch your sheet, and feel a sweat
Like water scalding from a pan,
And know the pain returning, yet
Its index absent on their scan,

To reach for hope, then taste the worst,
The gradual bursting of your joy,
When nothing works to summon thirst,
And anguish is its own alloy,

That would be easy, oh, for sure,
If you had even one year to live:
But the few words, *no final cure*,
Are all your doctors have to give.

So is it possible to go
Without the security of proof,
And lie, amidst the ill, below
The sterile bandage of this roof,

And smile, and eat your grapes, and see
Your daughters weeping, vague and lost,
And weep yourself, then smile at me,
And leave that last bridge still uncrossed?

Clearing His Room

So few things left: his last three pills
In a torn envelope; the plastic bowl
You tried to clean him in: dead flies there on the sill's

Brown varnish. And that little soul
Used up for ever like a pair of shoes
Thrown out. He left his earthy monuments, as a mole,

In blood and urine on old news,
Torn papers furnishing a sickroom floor.
His rectum was prolapsed. Pneumonia – choose

Which monster got him. From the door
I see the Gothic iron of the grate
He made his final den. There he would kneel, too sore

Even, at last, to evacuate
Rice water that you fed him from a syringe
Into the ash. But wanting to be clean, he'd wait

Until his bowels cleared. I cringe
To think of what his rear end must have been.
His lungs broke, and he couldn't cry. But, like a hinge

Creaking, he wheezed. He grew so lean
His back was like sharp winter roots of a tree
In the ground. But he retained some delicate gloss, or sheen,

In his fur. Prey of the wandering flea
And the inside worm, he died away from home
At the vet's. And this has changed Joanna's death for me.

The Leveret, in the Twilight

for Iseult

You found him beside the wall,
on his side, in the sun.

The long body laid sideways,
the great legs bent.

I touched what seemed the still-warm,
heaving fur,
watched the brown eyes, like small dates,
the black-tipped, fluted ears.

He was dying, even then.

I got a cardboard box
from the dairy,
and turned him over
to see if he was wounded.

There was only a trickle of urine,
like clear water.

We put him in the tack room
in the afternoon darkness
with the door locked against the dog.

He lay, without moving,
in a bed of straw and ruined leaves
balanced above the cold floor
on a set of folding deck-chairs.

And there he must have exhausted his coma,
and given back what was given to him
in his own time.

I don't know when.

He may even still be alive
as I write these lines,
hearing the rain beat on the south window
in the wind,
as the May night seeps in early,
the long season of spring dying
beginning as usual.

One last thing
I remember now
in the warmth of my study
is the way you crossed yourself
as if to avert what had to come.

I think of Cowper,
mourning his lovely pets.
I think of the little, round-nosed vole
the cats took this morning.

I think of that long darkness
creeping out of the west,
and of you, Iseult,
eight years old, on Tuesday,
who found a dying hare, in the sun,
for your birthday present.

A Thrush

Hung in a cat cage from the ceiling
  The thrush from Ashby Hall was fed
With snails and spiders, then crushed plum,
      But now is dead.

Plump when he came, but later thinner,
  He dangles on a long green rope
In an old blackbird's nest, with grasses,
      And there's no hope

He'll cheep again, as he did, ruffling
  His chestnut feathers to a ball
Or open his nut beak, or hear
      Grown thrushes call

Outdoors in laurel, or in ashes,
  And blink his little bead-like eye
And think of how, when he's much older,
      He'll learn to fly

And feed his crop with earwigs, aphids,
  And sing at sunset from a tree
Songs that will never tire or end
      At least for me.

The Place

Sometimes, if I look back, I see the road
And high suburban houses crowding down
Towards the gennel, and then Bingham Park
As a presence at the bottom, green with trees.
It makes a crescent, a strange rising curve
That loops back round in swallowing itself
Like a sort of buckled belt. Through each front door
The little hall runs through, and through the kitchen,
To a stone plateau, a kind of flight of steps
Protected by iron railings from the drop.
You could stand outside there, and look all round.
Nothing was happening, and everything.
But how much was real? I mean really real,
Enclosed all round by brick and pebbledash
With fences, dropping lawns, and shrubbery?
I don't know. Something blurs whatever comes,
And a kind of sad fear sifts between the stones.
I can't tell memories from photographs.
Granny in black, and Smuts, whoever Smuts was,
And my father's Humphrey-Bogart-looking hat,
They're all the same, determined by being in albums.
I have to start elsewhere, if anywhere.

In Hangingwater Road

There must have been a cliff, whose end
Was Endcliffe Park: and Westbourne Road
      Must once have showed
Where the sun set on something owned. My friend,

Ian, who was the first I knew
And measured cocks with, might have guessed.
      If he were pressed,
I wonder, would he shake sand from his shoe

And show the way? No, he would not.
There never, in our time, were bounds
      Where boys on rounds
With papers might have touched some foreign slot

And found the past. That lay aside,
Far back, and tasteless. Cold, unseen
      By any deft machine
That might manipulate the nerves of pride

And lay a country bare: a land
Out of the reach of he or I,
      Somewhere to cry
And summon swallows in, shake by the hand

The dead, the glorious ones, once more.
I mean my father, and his kind,
      The soldiers, blind
As always to the watchers on the shore.

There must have been a cataract
That fell, yet seemed to stay, years back.

It must have lacked
Some heaviness at heart, or, growing slack

In a tall place, dwindled, and stalled.
I write its name in wonder here
And let it steer
Its own sad course, apparelled, unappalled

In these late lines. I never found,
In those lost days, that waterfall,
Nor heard at all
Any sound of trickling trembling from the ground.

The hanging water failed. I showed
No interest, nor wet my feet
Wading to greet
That spirit sea in Hangingwater Road.

Sheffield surrounded me with wars
And daily chores. I grew and changed
And what had ranged
Inside my being, free, drained through my pores.

The First Things Read

William began it, nearly. Before him,
Only prehistory of animals,
Furred ears, and woodland murmurs, and big pages,
Grunt in the undergrowth of what I recall.
William was first. A holocaust of red

Where *The Dictator* and *The Gangster* ruled
And quantity was all. I boasted once
I'd read the whole bunch before I was eight.
Later books changed. Frail Ginger and the gang
Receded into cupboards. Violence came
With a face of battle, and a hope of honour,
In the wake of the war. I craved for bolder meat.
I don't remember who it was who wrote
Wings of Doom, that elemental read.
But still its villains, and their awful names,
Nicholas Trott, Red Barb, and Captain Shivers,
Francis Felkington Frapp, those rogues, these titles
Echo down the years. Air stories, yes,
With Biggles to the fore, and at the front,
Ruffled my days, and civilized my nights,
Once Richmal Crompton's William had been shelved.
School stories, though, were foremost. Why, I think
I know. It was their brutal ceremonies,
With beatings, rugby, and some pride of place.
Already the desire for grace was there,
Devouring Gunby Hadath. But Frank Richards,
He was the best, with his extremes of style,
Dragging the nineteenth century towards the forties
With bullies, Eton collars, and one hero,
Arthur Augustus D'Arcy, whom I adored.
I could be him. Slurred rs and monocle
Meant how a defect of the voice or eyes
Might give some poise of aristocracy
To a boy in Sheffield. So those treasured rags,
The yellow *Gems*, the orange *Magnets*, brought
Essence of glory into Southbourne Road.
I hoped the war might end, and bring them back.
It never did, that way. And I grew older
And cried for other friends. James Elroy Flecker
Lifted the veil, and brought the hopeless East

Into my mind, the exoticism of Damascus,
The secret floating of the nenuphars.
Tom Merry and his crowd went home to bed.

My Father's Patents

My father's patents in the dark,
Their red seals shining, show the way.
Black-framed they rise, on velvet ground,
And succour me, from hour to hour.

These, in a far day, made some mark,
Worked more for honour than for pay,
And what their dead inventor found
Lives on in me, as inward power.

This power I cherish. To it, I vow
Time to be honest, and try hard.
Let nothing violate them now,
These cream sheets that the washed plates guard.

I watch them in the crumbling dark
And hear the wind outside flow through
My torn acacia, blossoming white,
And the tombed, purple, hanging beech.

Here is a place for grief to park
And lie down, guiltless, by the yew
Whose bitter leaves bloom green tonight
And gather summer to their reach.

Summer, with rain. The last of June
Floods in the twilight of my south
And gives a sparkle to the spoon,
The living silver, in my mouth.

Born with such talent, years gone by,
Albeit wasted, seek repose,
And verse, weak as a butterfly,
Lifts from its chrysalis, and goes.

The Sewing-Room

I

Not here the way back to my mother's womb,
The echoed resonance of her last room.

I wonder why. The sewing-machine's the same
A Singer, or some other such. The lame

Tilt of the treadle, and the ironwork sides,
The set of plywood drawers, how each slides

And what they hold, these make a psychic link,
And filter Oby towards that Broomhill brink

Where all my mother's life surged up, then fell.
How could it happen? No one left can tell.

II

Sitting tonight here in the winter's cold
And warmed by a fan heater, I feel mould,

A sort of dankness of the soul, the ground
For cover, like a sort of creeping sound,

A taste of rancid butter, or a scent
Of rot in corners, or a sudden roughness, bent

On setting teeth on edge, the kind of sight
That makes the body shiver, halts the flight

Of sparrows, and grows ominous, and strange.
It gathers, like the soot that blacks a range.

III

But, fun of sorting! Three of them alike
In fake pearl, luminous, eyes of a pike

Plucked from the water of the running drawer
And, underneath, suspender-clasps, then floor,

A depth of sex, and fastening, fumbling hands
And whispered messages. Who understands?

Who wants to feel hot fingers loosening things?
The shifted stockings, or the restless rings

That turn and turn, in necklaces, on wrists,
And round the necks of virgins, with clenched fists?

IV

Drifting away, the mind, restored, returns,
And, high as fluting on my concrete urns,

The furniture of adolescence shifts
And, there in place, I see my mother's gifts,

The good things that she left me, all put back
And bright as once they were, free from all slack

And future reinstatement of my own,
A jewel-box to my wife, a Gecophone,

A walnut wardrobe, and a studded box
Removed, and sold. Oh sad, pre-emptive shocks!

V

Later, the same may happen here. Unseen,
This very sewing-room, this used machine

I lean my elbows on, may twist and fall
Through other, bored hands, and may snap, and crawl

On fated ironwork ankles to the dump
Where men pick over mattresses, the rump

Of a dead sale, burned up, or thrown away,
Or left for dull abuse, another day,

And there lie down and die, without one voice
To plead for its return, or make that choice.

So I, the heir, at least must try to spare
The little past I feel thread through the air

And send me filtered echoes: here in holes
Through buttons, like their perforated souls,

Where what is empty can leak through, and sigh
To the finger's touch as absence, and where I,

Seeing the thread, may break it on my tongue,
And, with some giant effort, once more young,

Draw on the torn-off buttons, tie their ends,
And, where I can, sew back, and make amends.

She would have done the same. I mean for me,
If I had been the one to sink, and flee

In the face of pain, and dying. Loyal truth
Demands the same for age, as once from youth,

And what our parents mean, as force and time,
Never depends on any glint of rhyme

Or special resonance in what they are.
It glitters like a providential star.

It burns for ever, like an unhealed scar.
It forms our ground, hard granite, under tar.

In Love with Red

For years, I liked it least.
     It seemed so bold,
Strident and brassy, tinny at the worst,
A colour for the crude, the flashy ones,
     A slavering beast
  Of the palette, raging flame with gold,
     Something to burst
The eardrums, and explode like firework suns.

Now I know better. Home
     After three days
Of living in the meekness of dull stone
That London is, I turn to praise pure red.
     Seeing you comb
  A line of carmine to a glaze
     I want to atone
To all scarlet richness for my former dread.

I've come of age. This heat
     Of hue, that flares
In uniforms and holocausts, needs time.
Such blood of poppies by the late June roads!
     Now as I meet
  Red everywhere, with flagrant stares,
     Watching it climb,
I grant its depth, pulse leaping like a toad's.

At our party, I'll wear red,
     Mess-red with gold,
And flaunt amongst the rest, red's paladins.
I'll be an acolyte of vivid hue,
     And let the dead

Lie dim and simple in their cold.
A time for grins
Is come, for jousting crimson, all things new.

The 1914 Party

Across the lawn a long parade of girls
With buttoned gloves convey unpassing time
And underneath the beech, a wide skirt swirls:
Far out, like rhyme.

Dressed as a major in some abstruse corps
With Sam Browne belt, and crowns upon my sleeves
I slap my bulging cords, not worn before.
No one believes

My kind of officer. No pips or gun,
Or any polish on his riding-boots,
And my sword frog and flask are worn for fun.
If someone shoots,

His make believe loud shell will make a bang
And faze the ladies, twirling parasols.
Not one of us could march a parasang
Or fill with holes

A can of beer set up upon a cart
At fifty yards. I stroll, and would salute,
Though rather warily, what might impart
A distant hoot

Of laughter, a real military man,
This proper major, eighty-six years old,
Stiff on his stick, with keen eyes and a tan,
　　　Whose fire's grown cold.

Medals come easy, like this DSO
Whose colours nip my undeserving chest.
But his were his. Yes, that was long ago,
　　　And that seems best.

But still, inside my head, becapped and grey
With middle age, I think a fine salute
And make it stick. We play a game today
　　　But it takes root.

And in my mind, remembering that war
My father died in, and the one that's done,
Or may be done, this game is played with awe.
　　　And what's begun

In quirky humour, ends as reverence.
The women furl their things. It starts to rain.
And the Edwardian age, bought for some pence
　　　And a frill train,

Is drawn indoors. There sepia photographs
Of Wilfred Owen, and of Hemingway,
Who wears his helmet proudly, but still laughs,
　　　Preserve our play

And set it in a frame. I turn and pour
Another glass of port for someone new
In ordinary clothes, who likes my floor
　　　And wants the loo.

Over and changed, while even aeroplanes
Drawl slower than they should, and time withdraws
Into an age of flounces and balloons
Where huge full globes drop gently from tall skies
And settle near your eyes of open blue
That watch them in their easy capering,
    You will be known;

And being known, I say, as any child
While serendipity befits the year
With sound appraisals, and fair destiny,
Discarding veils of her auspiciousness,
Lets entrails and watched tea-leaves off the hook,
Knowing things well, while heat gives way to rain,
And, near the solid solstice, every plant
Shudders and rinses out its sweating clothes,
    You will be mine;

And being mine, you will be hers, whom I
Remember in the chill of our spring wood
As narrow as a poplar in the wind
And dark as claret in her flying suit;
There she picks bluebells, and the fine gnats rise
In twilight like an aureole round her hair
Of living wings, and she is cold and comes,
Arms full of flowers for vases, towards the house.
    You will be ours,

And being ours, while feathers of dry frost
Settle upon the elbows of each oak
And drown as manacles to ice their knees,
While hailstones pester beeches, that bear age
Like elephants, and toe the horny ground,
And ground itself, that loved the squeeze of feet
And now, grave harbinger, in fief to snow

Can neither offer space, nor warmth, to shoes,
    You will be grown;

And being grown, but not too soon, I hope,
Into a creature of some grace and power,
With skill and wisdom, and a temperament
Not too remote, perhaps, from those I know
And bear in others, tolerant, amused,
Incisive or withdrawn, in speech and ways
Deliberate or casual, boy or girl,
In knickerbockers, or in plaits and jeans,
    You will return;

And so, returned, and in your later prime,
As all must be who leave, while time grows old
And acorns pimp like nipples in the frost
And fertile mushrooms rot in roots of elms,
Carried at ease, and in no summer boat
From broad to fen, and so to that far creek
Where you began, where naked willows dress
Remainders of grey hair in muddy pools,
    You will seem lost;

And seeming lost, and in your disparate mood
Thrown from the windows of that tenement
I call my will, while hawthorn blossoms fall
Onto the road, and daffodils break wind
With yellow bellowing, and chestnut blossoms grope
Towards the final fir of flowering,
Near to some access of a private grief
That nothing understands but inward ire,
    You will break free;

And breaking free, while sleet bereaves the glass
That might recover from its muddy panes

Touch of your hands tacky with marmalade,
And while the Ural and branch-breaking wind
Arm-wrestles with each amnesty of oak
Along the frontiers of the farm, twisting
And elder, as that wizened tree, inside
The warped and sombre timbers of your brain,
    You will be changed;

And being changed, and growing in that change
Towards a different being, while the keys
Hang on each sycamore, and emerald heads,
Grisly with spikes, break to mahogany
And load the wood's floor with their conquering seeds,
And autumn in the air, that ancient sage,
Parades fertility with failing rust,
Opening doors that never closed before,
    You will grow sad;

And growing sad, and comforted perhaps
Beside the arches and the cracked brick walls
Of that small chapel, you will sleep and dream;
And dreaming, while, from unmolested clouds
The quiet rain slips to each parted leaf
And moistens your white cuffs, and wets your face
That knows all things in secret, as the seed
The heart, you will feel loved, my child, I swear,
    You will feel loved.

To Alexander, Sleeping

A little soldier watches through your cot
    In a black busby, and red coat.
    His outstretched arms, wedged through the cane,
Attract your eye, perhaps, as these things can.

I wonder, though. While dozing, both eyes shut,
    Against the towel of your sheet,
    Have you, alongside your left knee,
Another soldier, whom you never knew,

Living in how the flesh bends, and the hair
    Drifts backwards from the warm skull here?
    I like to think so. And that soon
These echoes of his time that kept me sane,

The faltering mementoes of my drawer,
    When shown to you, will not seem drear
    Or meaningless, but something prized,
And by your gesturing, fine hands appraised.

The night that you were born, an unknown nurse
    Knitted this present. It seemed nice
    At first, and now more real, though frail,
Than any lace around your cot, or frill.

A soldier for a soldier. This for one
    Whose fingers of a Scottish wain
    Can grasp the softness of a war
And learn what heritage he has to wear.

My father's uniform was dull as mud
    Not like this pretty wool one made

394

In colours, but of khaki serge
Whose beaten honours no grief can assuage.

I tell you, Alexander, my young son,
    Whose body now must keep me sane,
    That one day later, bound by blood,
Your conscience will salute all those who bled,

And there, amongst them, cherish your near line
    By being what you are, alone
    Out of that massive sea, your clan,
The one remaining soldier, weak and clean.